LEAD AND LET LIVE

www.amplifypublishinggroup.com

Lead and Let Live: Leadership Lessons for the Future of Work

For more information, please contact:
Amplify Publishing, an imprint of Amplify Publishing Group
620 Herndon Parkway, Suite 320
Herndon, VA 20170
info@amplifypublishing.com

Library of Congress Control Number: 2022908933

CPSIA Code: PRV1222A

ISBN-13: 978-1-63755-493-7

Printed in the United States

To my children, Kyle and Madeleine.

lead
AND LET
live

Leadership Lessons
for the Future of Work

BARBIE BREWER

an imprint of Amplify Publishing Group

CONTENTS

FOREWORD

WE HAVE ALL HEARD THAT life is a journey. Many believe that the journey is just as important as the destination.

Perhaps. But since life involves more than one journey and more than one purpose, a wise person also comes to understand that life is also a matter of gaining perspective. Along the way, the most ambitious of us ask many questions because we believe the right answers can make the journey more successful.

As we acquire perspective, we tend to ask more questions of ourselves than others. The right answers can make our life meaningful and, importantly, *helpful to others*.

Among the questions we ask are: Just how precious is our time? How important are our career accomplishments? What will our legacy be? And, of course, why?

Lead and Let Live by the accomplished Barbie Brewer is a journey in perspective that also provides us with compelling answers as to why.

Barbie's successful journeys include important career positions at IBM, GitLab, and Netflix, where she helped develop a work culture that was recognized nationally as transformative.

Barbie's rising star provided her with accolades and even

fortune. Yet, like so many others, she was forced in life to make the stark admission that "it took a crisis to force me to focus on what's important in life." That crisis, which came in the form of cancer, gave her the perspective in life lessons from which we all can now benefit.

By weaving everyday personal experiences, with difficulties and triumphs both slight and traumatic, Barbie accelerates our journey into greater perspective.

"You don't have to have all the answers yet," she assures us. "You just need to be willing to engage in the search for them." As we step into this understanding, we also come to understand, as she did, that "growth lives *beyond* the comfort zones." Within the corporate world, she explains, growth also requires that we "take chances on *each other*."

But don't read *Lead and Let Live* just to become a better executive or team leader or more successful in your career. While she will help you do that, read this book to realize the greatest legacy of a leader and person lies in the gift of *meaning* that you give not just to your co-workers but also to your family, children, and friends.

Finally, perhaps the greatest of artists, Michelangelo, favored sculpture far more than painting because stone gave a lasting permanence to his art that the stroke of a brush simply could not. With this book, Barbie Brewer gives all of us lasting meaning that transcends simple success.

That is a journey we should all jump at the chance to get on board to experience.

THOMAS G. DEL BECCARO
Author, *The Divided Era*
Opinion writer and commentator at Fox News/Fox Business

The Origin Story

SOMETHING YOU'LL LEARN VERY QUICKLY about me as you begin this book is that I am brutally honest. I believe that honesty is essential in both leadership and life, and since my book will focus on both, it is fitting and appropriate to begin with an honest admission: I've never been much of a writer.

This might sound a strange coming from a now-published author, but I share this admission right up front because of its contextual and historical significance. The fact of the matter is that I've always been more of an *oral* communicator. As an executive who speaks to audiences of hundreds and even thousands of people all over the world, verbal communication had always been my preference, my passion, and my most comfortable mode of expression. Public speaking, for me, is second nature, whether I'm facilitating a workshop on executive leadership, coaching a group of CEOs, or training HR professionals to support remote teams.

Until my life changed.

After being diagnosed with a "Desmoid" tumor, a rare sarcoma, I was suddenly facing the very raw possibility that my two children, then eleven and nine, might be forced to grow up without me. In the twinkling of an eye—the time it took to receive the diagnosis and the none-too-promising prognosis—I became a mother who probably wouldn't live to see her children evolve into teenagers, then college students, then full-blown adults with children of their own. As it concerned my two children, the long and short of it was this: they wouldn't have me, and I wouldn't have them. There was the very real chance that I'd never see my daughter walk across the stage and give a proud "I did it!" fist pump at her college graduation, nor would I ever have the experience of snapping that all-important photo of my son and his date as they posed in our hallway before heading off to prom. Never would I hold (or even say hello to) my yet-unborn grandkids, little lives who will one day share my blood and continue my legacy.

Or at least that was the scenario that was staring me down at the time. The heartbreaking truth, as I looked down the barrel of this diagnosis, was that I would never know the beautiful adult human beings my beautiful children would grow up to be—a scenario no mother on this planet should ever have to face. But there it was, the unthinkable possibility before me, like a dark, gaping chasm in my soul.

This is when I picked up my pen and started writing. This is when the written word took on new significance for me; when my written words became the vehicle and the vessel through which I could pour my wisdom and my maternal guidance into the minds and hearts of my little ones in a way that would hopefully prove to be enduring and relevant long after I was gone.

At that time, the stakes were high and time was short, which meant that every word I wrote needed to be exactly right. These words were going to stand in my place after I left this world, so it was imperative they be straightforward, comforting, firm, compassionate, and courageous. These were to be the words that would fill in for me in my absence, so they needed to count. I owed my children at *least* that much.

In the midst of this setback that rocked my world and made me reevaluate all that was important to me, I actually wrote my children many goodbye letters. I suppose you could say a *series* of letters, really, that conveyed the progress of my life over a series of days, years, and decades. Important milestones and pivotal moments that evolve into memories do not happen all at once; they unfold gradually, as life itself unfolds. In writing these letters, I wanted to share with them important life lessons and maternal wisdom that would guide them through the various stages and phases of life. I wanted to share my thoughts about how to navigate the ups and downs of high school, for instance, or what to do when they experienced their first heartbreak (hint: respect the pain for what it is, but ultimately, push through that pain because, frankly, *not* pushing through is not an option). I wanted to share words about how to treat others (always with respect and kindness), and words about how to be and become the kind of human that others want to be and become.

I wanted my letters to create the sensation (or maybe the illusion) that I was right there with them, guiding them and protecting them as they rode the waves of life's most challenging situations, just like my own mother had always been there for me. As a child, my mother's presence in my life was as sure and as steady as a heartbeat; never once did she falter in her unconditional love and support for me and my older sister. One time, for example, I told her that I wanted to be a model, a pathologist, and a lawyer when I grew up, and she told me I could easily be all three. It didn't matter to me whether she believed I could do it. What mattered is that she believed in *my belief* that I could do it! My mom was encouraging me, of course, with her assurance that I could easily achieve this unusual trifecta ... but she was also instilling in me the first wisps of self-confidence, self-awareness, and tenacity. Ultimately, I never pursued any of those three options, but that was irrelevant to my mom. The only thing she cared about was that I knew she was in my corner, regardless of whatever career or life choices I made. No matter what curve balls life threw me, she was there for me. Always.

I believe that all children deserve that kind of unconditional, unrelenting support and encouragement from their parents, simply because life itself will be discouraging enough for them as they get older. Even today, my mother is my best friend and closest confidant. In fact, in writing these words, I realized that, in some ways, the certainty and solidity of my own mother's presence in my life when I was a child made it even more difficult for me to embrace the possibility that I might not be able to be there for my own kids. The contrast was heartbreakingly stark: my mother was there for me in a way that I probably would not be there for them. However, as I was writing these goodbye letters, something significant began to happen: a gradual, graceful dawning within me, as bright and as luminous as the rising sun.

Here's what I realized. The lessons I was leaving for my children about human resilience, humility, survival, honesty, adaptability, integrity, grit, gratitude, and so on, might also resonate with and bring benefit to a wider audience.

This is when the idea of writing a book that encapsulates these life lessons slowly began to take shape. These were lessons that could prove to be sustainable and enduring not just for my children, but for people I've never known or met—readers like you, and perhaps your colleague, your neighbor (if you pass this book along, that is!)—who might benefit from these practical principles about life and living. What, then, started as a deeply intimate form of communication between a mother and her two young children, gradually morphed into an all-encompassing message from which many, many more souls could benefit. This is my hope, anyway.

In a sense, this universal concept is still familial. How? Because the lessons herein were originally crafted for my children are now shared with you, my brothers and sisters with whom I live in the larger world. Aren't we all part of a human "family," in the most expansive sense of the word? And isn't it true that the actions we take and the decisions we make as leaders will either contribute to or compromise the well-being of this world we share as a *global* family? I strongly believe that the answers to both these questions are "yes." Do you agree?

From there I started thinking about work itself, about how so many of the messages in this book—and in the letters that I wrote to my children—will resonate deeply with readers who are searching for ways to make their organizations better to work for.

I also realized that it was time to share some of the important lessons I've learned from amazing leaders I've worked with throughout my career. These lessons are enduring, and they have had a profound impact on the person and the leader I have become. In a very real way, the leaders I've learned from are fully present in this book, because their wisdom still lives within me.

This is what leaders do: we inform each other with our experiential wisdom. This is how we learn, how we grow, how we become better leaders!

As I began conceiving and developing the idea of this book, I thought about how useful a tool it might be for leaders and executives of all kinds who genuinely want to change their leadership paradigm so that it becomes more meaningful and more sustainable. If you are that leader, I want you to be able to use this book as a roadmap to guide yourself along on your journey.

I also thought about the fact that life and work unavoidably overlap. There is no such thing as the "perfect balance," nor do we want there to be, really. A separation of life and work cannot be surgically precise. To succeed, we must work hard at living! We must put in the work professionally and personally. Success doesn't happen by a process of spontaneous combustion; it is a purposeful process. I've spent much of my career in executive leadership roles, maneuvering at the highest pinnacles of corporate and managerial success, and every one of the principles and character traits we'll explore in this book have been (and still are) responsible for my career growth and advancement. Put simply, these lessons are transferable. They manifest beautifully in everyday life, but *they also apply in the workplace*. My hope is that you can shape and mold these shared concepts in a way that allows them to manifest in your own life, too.

Within this book, therefore, you will find a healthy combination of lessons on life and lessons on leadership, because the two really do go hand in hand. The themes we'll explore in each chapter will offer leadership principles for the next generation of entrepreneurs to consider as they shape their own styles and make their own way, but we'll also explore these lessons in a more expansive sense, in a more human-centered, "daily life" sense, which will speak to every reader, no matter their background, education, career path, or area of specific interest. These will be life principles and work principles—and perhaps work-life principles—that will help light the way for *all* of us as we try to lead productive, meaningful, sustainable lives.

With the same sense of urgency that I wanted to use my written words to guide my children on a path they might have had to walk without me, I also want to share these concepts and principles with you, too. I strongly believe that we must all do our part to make this world—both our working world and the planet upon which we live—a better place. All of us have a role. All of us must play a part.

To that end, chapter by chapter, we'll examine the elements that comprise successful leadership and responsible living on a vast human scale. From the chapter titled "Take a Chance," that suggests you must take a chance on yourself if you want others to take a chance on you, to the chapter "The Virtuous Circle of Leadership," which asserts that paying it forward is not just a pleasant saying but a purposeful act, my hope is that humanity lives within the pages of this book. A humanity based on my personal and professional experiences can be customized and retrofitted into your own life in a way that makes the most sense to you.

The best way to describe this book is deeply experiential and deliberately nonjudgmental. I will draw from the depths of my own human experience and share with you some of the highlights of what I've learned throughout my career and the course of my life. I share these lessons humbly, with grace and gratitude.

To be sure, I am profoundly grateful to have beaten the odds and made it through my illness. (Let me rephrase that: I didn't just "make it through," I *pushed* through, persevered, and fought like hell to survive and, today, to thrive.) I am grateful, too, to have survived and thrived in the midst of corporate cutbacks, reorgs, divorce, startups, shutdowns, snags, victories, defeats, and so many unexpected factors that bubble up during the course of living life. In fact, without these challenges, I wouldn't be where (and who) I am today, so I choose to count everything as a blessing rather than a setback.

Without going through what I've gone through—without experiencing all that I have experienced as a woman, a mother, an executive, an entrepreneur, an industry leader, and a human being who lives, eats, breathes just like you do—I wouldn't be who I am today. Yes, it took a crisis to force me to focus on what's important in life, and I mean *really* focus with laser-like intensity, but don't we usually end up learning the most enduring lessons from our darkest moments? Search your heart and see if you agree. If you've experienced crisis in your life (who amongst us hasn't?), you know what I'm talking about. Within those dark moments, silver linings can always be found; you just have to look for them. I, for one, always tend to find them.

My goals for this book are simple: I want these lessons to endure; I want to share them in a way that will make a qualitative difference in your life and in the lives of others; I want these words to resonate in a way that will help make leaders more responsible, entrepreneurs more courageous, young people more confident, communities more connected; and, ultimately, to help make the world a better place in which to live and work. What started as a series of goodbye letters to my two children has evolved into what I hope will be a book that infuses new energy into not-so-new conversations about principle-centered leadership, expanding opportunity, organizational success, human decency, and compassionate, responsible, purposeful living.

If you're looking for new ways to lead, for fresh ways to focus on issues like organizational change and the redistribution of opportunity, or even if you're seeking some simple guidance on how to become the very best version of yourself, join me on this journey. I hope you can sense my outstretched hand. Reach out and take hold of it now so that our journey can begin. Not tomorrow. Not next month. Not the second you cross off that last task on your to-do list. Let's begin together. *Now.*

I will not strongarm you. I will not lecture. These are living lessons designed to inspire, motivate, and maybe even drive you to action. There will be no edicts delivered from on high, no lofty lessons that flutter down from the sky. These lessons will come from the depth of my own experiences—straightforward, honest, and sometimes raw.

I will meet you where you are.

We will walk together.

1

Always Make Time to Dance

I WANT EACH LESSON I SHARE in this book, whether a lesson about life or a lesson about leadership, to have humanity, a heartbeat. Each story, anecdote, and experience I share must have a pulse. That's why it's important for me to begin, well, at the beginning, to take you back so that these lessons can unfold, in your mind, from a place of deeper context. I want to share a little about my past, right at the beginning of this book not least because these pieces of my past make up the person and leader I am today.

In fact, it might be a useful exercise, as you evaluate your own path forward, to reflect on how the memories, moments, and experiences from your own past have helped mold and define the person you are today. There is power in the past; it offers us a useful guidepost moving forward and reminds us that where we are standing today, and where we are going tomorrow, is often guided (but never dictated, thankfully) by where we've been.

I share some of these early experiences, too, because there are living lessons within them that I'm hopeful—no, *confident*—will be of use to you in your own life in some way. That is the purpose of this book, after all: To share these lessons in a way that will somehow bring value and enduring wisdom to your own work and leadership life.

So, we begin at the beginning.

Facing Down the Boogeymen

I grew up in Modesto, California. My mom was a teacher, and my father was a CFO who later quit to become a truck driver. Looking back on it now, I realize that many of the leadership characteristics that drive me today were born during those early years of my life.

Even as a child, for instance, I remember teaching myself to be unhesitant and unafraid: two vital characteristics of a successful leader. It should be noted that being unhesitant isn't the same as acting without careful forethought, which is a distinction that's important for leaders to make. Second, with regard to being unafraid, decisiveness and courage aren't always innate: they can be acquired or honed. Just because you're not *born* brave and bold doesn't mean you can't *become* brave and bold. Good news, to be sure.

My sister Kathie helped hone my courage without even realizing it. Kathie was a little afraid of the dark. Many nights, I'd sing her songs and check her closet for the boogeyman if we came home after dark (because what child isn't at least a little scared of the boogeyman, including yours truly?). And whenever we went to the amusement park, she'd ask me to ride the roller coaster first, before she would get on, "just to make sure it was okay." Never mind that I was two years younger! Never mind that I might have felt fear and hesitation stirring in my *own* little heart every time I pulled that closet door open to check for boogeymen or hopped into the rickety car of a roller coaster that would take me high, high up into the air. I automatically took on the role of the risk-taker (even though I wasn't naturally that way inclined) or the brave protector from the boogeyman (even though I often felt afraid) because it was the right thing to do.

Don't get me wrong—Kathie was (and remains) strong, spirited, and fiercely independent. She taught me the importance of speaking up and advocating for myself. Even when we were kids, she taught me vital lessons about life, even about leadership, that I carry with me to this to very day. It's just that she was afraid of the dark and of roller coasters, and because I loved her, I wanted to do whatever I could do lessen her fears.

> The leadership lesson here is that even if you feel a little hesitant or a little afraid of doing something that you know must be done for the greater good, push yourself to do it anyway. Eventually, both the fear and the hesitancy subside.

Leaders and readers, remember this: your employees don't expect you to be perfect, but they expect you to lead. And part of being an effective leader means doing those things, making those decisions, facilitating those changes, that will bring benefit to your organization, even if it feels a little uncomfortable, even scary getting there.

Looking back on it now, I'm very glad I opened that closet door, rode all those roller coasters, and sang all those nighttime songs to my sister, simply because it made her feel less afraid. It made her feel a little better about the world around her and her place within it. Isn't this what the people within our organizations want as well? To feel comfortable and confident about the company they work for and their place within it? After all, the humans within our organizations play a vital role in determining the future direction of companies and define and strengthen our organizations' cultures, but those of us at the helm must guide this process. Those of us who are leaders must lead.

We must lead with courage and with clarity. Isn't that what leadership is all about?

Girls in Scouting: Purpose Driven, Then and Now

Even though I had my share of wild moments during high school, I was, more often than not, predictable and purpose driven. I always found school easy, but I still worked hard at everything I did. For me, high school was all about getting into college; I even joined the Boy Scouts in high school because they had a work-shadowing program that allowed scouts to gain insight into people's careers and professions. Today, the group is referred to as just "Scouts," and it embraces all young people, regardless of gender (we should all take a page from that playbook), but at the time, I didn't advertise my scout membership broadly to my friends for fear of ridicule, and fortunately for me, there was never a formal requirement to attend meetings, but I did enjoy the membership benefits. Being able to see and speak with people who were already comfortable, confident, and established in their careers was something that helped pave my own leadership path: you need to see what you want to become.

In every leadership and/or executive position I've ever held, I always tried to make myself accessible to those who might be looking for motivation, inspiration, and a clear view of what leadership truly *looks* like. We owe our young people at least that much since they will be the ones not only following in our footsteps but also charting new courses. They need to see at least one version (ours) of how things work. Even if they decide to diverge from the path trodden before them (which is how progress happens), they at least need to see that a path existed.

My advice to leaders is, to the extent that you can, make a concerted, sustained effort to allow your new, less experienced employees to shadow you. Let them see what they can one day become; give them something to aspire to. It opens up their world and expands their perspective. It certainly expanded mine. It also makes good business sense, because young employees and new minds approach projects and potential problems from a fresh, untarnished perspective, and fresh perspective is a necessary ingredient for change. On the flip side, though, it's as important that employees see you make mistakes as it is for them to see your victories, triumphs, and successes. Valuable lessons can be learned from our missteps and failures . . . as long as we don't keep making those same mistakes over and over! That's what leadership is all about: learning and growing from both your successes and your failures.

Working Hard, Playing Hard

I graduated *magna cum laude* from Santa Clara University with a major in communications and a minor in business. SCU is a small, private Jesuit school that drew me to it for a number of non-religious reasons, among them that it had an excellent academic reputation, small classes, and brilliant professors who were totally dedicated to teaching. Like my attitude in high school, I approached college with a sense of purpose, but here's a new flash about this thing called "purpose-driven intensity"... such intensity doesn't stop you having fun or squeezing out every smidgen of joy you possibly can from each and every day and, in my case, most nights.

I'll tell you what I mean. My very first job was at Exodus Communications, a fast-growing network management company in Silicon Valley, where I worked as a marketing communications coordinator. I was also a full-time student, taking twenty units a quarter. So, my life was busy, to say the least. But being busy was never daunting to me, nor was it a burden or distraction. It was par for the course. It's how I *lived*. After working and going to classes each day, both on a full-time basis, I'd turn my attention towards other activities that brought me joy. Though work and school were obviously important, I wasn't going to let either of them stop me from squeezing as much fun and enjoyment out of my life as I possibly could. I didn't see life as a zero-sum game, nor did I see it as a series of either-or possibilities. Purpose and passion can definitely coexist: yet another important leadership lesson.

I've always loved dancing and music, so after working and going to school each day, I'd go out dancing in the evening. From about 7:00 PM until about 2:00 AM, my life was all about line dancing, country dancing, swing—you name it, I danced it. Was it a lot to handle? Of course it was! But being as purposeful about my passions (music and dancing were just two of them) was as important to me as being purposeful about my pursuit of both education and gainful employment. None of it was mutually exclusive. Why on earth *should* it be?

I threw myself totally and completely into everything I did. To this very day, I still do. If you're not going to throw 100 percent of yourself into whatever project or passion is before you, why even bother involving yourself in at all? In everything, try to give it your best shot, your most monumental effort; nothing else will do.

A healthy, holistic way to live life and evolve into a successful human-centered leader is to simply work hard at work and work hard at having fun. Here's another way to say it: give *all* of it your all.

Genesis at Exodus

While I was at Exodus, when it was a young company expanding at a meteoric rate, I learned my first important lessons about corporate growth, namely that one must be smart about growth.

Working for a fast-growing company is a *lifestyle*; it's a commitment. I was lucky to be working at an organization that was growing at the speed of light—especially as my first job—and to learn the important lesson that growth simply for the sake of growth should not necessarily be the goal. Yes, growing fast is great . . . but growing *smart* is even better. Growing fast *and* growing smart is the ideal combination, of course. Exodus was strategic and purposeful in its growth, which taught me to be strategic and purposeful in my own growth as a human; a great lesson to learn at such a young age, when life still stretched out before me like an open road.

Working at Exodus also taught me that with growth must come flexibility and adaptability; that change is inevitable, so honing a spirit of resilience is mandatory; and don't sweat the small stuff. I still carry these lessons with me today, and they live within my own leadership style.

I also teach these principles to CEOs and executives throughout the world. I teach them that, in both leadership and in life, it is important to set a clear goal and a precise purpose but to remember that purpose-driven leadership can and should *also* include a whole lot of joy along the way. Success takes hard work, and hard work takes constant commitment, but don't forget to seek joy during your pursuit. Remarkably, I've known lots of leaders who actually *fear* fun. I've worked with CEOs and top execs who operate under the assumption that if they're having too much fun, they're not working hard enough. I am always quick to disabuse them of this notion and, invariably, they are always grateful to have been steered towards a more expansive understanding of what it means to better integrate work and life. Life is not just about work, and work is not all that there is to life. The two must coexist.

Are you currently trying to establish a healthier, more fulfilling balance between your life as a serious-minded, highly engaged leader and yourself as a well-rounded, fully developed human being? Perhaps consider taking a page from the very first playbook I developed during my college days, because it still holds true to this very day: at the end of day, always make time to dance.

Be the Flame

Another self-defining position that I held early in my career was at IBM, where I managed the internship program for the eleven western US states. Not a bad gig for someone in their early twenties.

At Exodus, I focused on marketing, but this job at IBM represented my first real foray into the human resources space. The switch from marketing to HR felt right; I felt comfortable and, equally important, *confident* standing within this new space. I took to it right away. The switch, for me, was important because it taught me that trying new things and dipping my toe into new areas of expertise is the right and the wise thing to do. Ultimately, this was to be far more than toe-dipping, and people-centered HR space is where I have remained in some form or fashion throughout my career.

The job at IBM also represented the first time a company *invested* in me, that is made me feel a valued and valuable member of the team. They flew me out to their headquarters in White Plains, New York, for extensive training, taking a chance on this "rookie" because they saw something in me that I hadn't yet seen in myself. Leaders, listen up: investing in your young people and giving them solid training is the smartest thing you'll ever do. So, do it.

Here's the thing about bringing in young people to your company. Of course it can be risky because they're still new to everything and don't even know what they don't know yet. This makes the process of interviewing them for the job challenging as well . . . I know because I've probably interviewed thousands of people throughout my HR career. But even in the interviewing process, you can be smart about risk. For example, instead of asking a young potential recruit where they see themselves in five or ten years, ask them how they'd figure out a problem or navigate a specific challenge. Would they seek the guidance of their manager every step of the way or would they be confident enough to at least consider a potential solution of their own? Smart interviewing requires training, dexterity, and discernment, to be sure. This is why your HR people and hiring managers need to be well trained. This, too, is a wise investment.

It was my subsequent job at Cisco, however, that guided my career trajectory *and* my life in a serious, substantial way. I was still managing interns in the same way I had at IBM, but my slice of the pie was now much bigger. My territory was no longer confined to eleven states; it had expanded to the entire nation. Cisco also paid for my master's degree, and obtaining my master's enhanced my life experience and expanded the depth and breadth of my knowledge in immeasurable ways. It was also the first time an *individual* stepped up, singled me out, and identified my potential in a way that I hadn't identified yet. It's one thing for a company to throw their resources behind you as one of many in the organizational pack; it's another thing entirely for one person, a devoted executive within a company, to see something within you that you don't even see yourself and to throw their weight behind you in a way that changes the entire trajectory of your personal and professional life. Looking back over my career, I realize I've played that kind of motivational role for hundreds (if not thousands) of young people. To the extent that you can in your own leadership life, try to be the spark that ignites both confidence and courage in your new hires. Be their flame.

My flame had a name: Kate DeCamp. Kate was head of HR at Cisco at the time. It was Kate who gave me the solid grounding I needed and the opportunities to fully stretch out into the professional HR space. And when I say "stretch," I *really* mean stretch. At a company softball game one bright afternoon, Kate, who'd come to watch her daughter play, looked me in the face and asked, "Would you ever consider taking an international assignment with the company?"

Remember that lesson I described at the very beginning of this chapter about teaching yourself to be unhesitant, especially when it's for the greater good or for when opportunity for growth and advancement comes knocking? Well, that lesson really kicked into high gear for me at that moment, because my answer to Kate was as swift as it was certain: "Yes! I'd consider an international assignment in a *heartbeat*," I told her, even though my heart was hammering a million times a minute. Of course, I played it cool. Sure enough, very shortly after my encounter with Kate, I was called into a meeting to discuss the possibility of working in Europe. Two months later, my fiancé and I were flying across the Atlantic, on our way to live on another continent.

During discussions about which country I would be assigned to, Kate had asked me if I spoke any languages, and I told her I spoke French. She made the counterintuitive decision not to send me to France because, after all, where's the growth in that? Why send someone to a French-speaking country when she can already speak French? So, she sent me to Germany instead.

I learned countless lessons from the spirited and direct Ms. DeCamp, and she remains a good friend to this very day. But among the most important takeaway is to show your employees you believe in them with your actions, then push them beyond comfort zones. Why?

Because growth lives *beyond* the comfort zones.

Netflix Nirvana

I can't reflect in any meaningful way about the enduring leadership lessons I've learned throughout my career without reflecting on my experience working as an executive at Netflix. And yes, the descriptor in the subheading is the adjective I'd use to describe the entirety of my experience there: "Nirvana." You can probably tell by now that I am not the type of person who relies on hyperbole. I'm generally a straightshooter and a plain speaker, so my use of the superlative is not only rare but, in this particular case, entirely appropriate.

Netflix was (and still is) filled with amazing people with extraordinary talent and tremendous creative drive. My coworkers were brave and brilliant, and every single one of them was someone I could—and did—learn from. I was in my early thirties when I started at the company, and right away I could tell that they knew how to hire the right people. I could tell that the CEO was confident enough in himself to drive hiring decisions down to the lowest levels of the company in a way that would ensure that the operational managers were both autonomous and accountable, and that this was a company that *put their people first*.

The other amazing thing about Netflix, from an organizational and HR perspective, was that they *believed* in their people. This was the first large company I'd ever worked for that didn't do performance reviews, which taught me something important. I learned that if you hire the right people, you don't need to micromanage their progress. Instead, you trust them to make the best decisions, to do the right and equitable thing, and to always act in the interest of the company.

No amount of bureaucracy or paper-shuffling can trump trust. It is not necessary for the HR department to develop a multi-page policy manual to protect the company against the mismanagement of funds or to teach employees how to avoid making dumb decisions. You simply don't hire people who do that ... or you fire them if they're already there and the missteps persist. You fix the problem. Period.

At Netflix, I learned the *caliber of talent* is paramount and each and every human within an organization should be fully seen and celebrated as being valued and valuable. As the HR professional who interviewed each new or potential employee before they were brought on board, I saw with my own eyes that the threads of fierce commitment to culture fit, to excellence, and to experience were woven into every conceivable aspect of the company. My experience there was singularly unique ... as were the circumstances of my departure.

We Need to Run More Tests

In many ways, my time at Netflix coincided with a strange and very intense confluence of events within my personal life, a perfect storm, that eventually mandated a change in my life and my lifestyle.

For one, I filed for divorce. I had two children by then, so the divorce suddenly threw me into the world of single motherhood. And here, a shoutout to single mothers everywhere: I *see* you. I see you working and balancing and being the very best version of yourselves that you can possibly be for your children. I see the sacrifices you make and the strength within you. I thank you for imparting so much of that strength to me when I needed it most, and for inspiring me when I needed to see other single mothers kicking butt and living their lives with courage and conviction. To single moms everywhere, I offer my admiration and great gratitude.

During my time at Netflix, the perfect storm that was unfolding in my personal life became increasingly tumultuous. Both my small children, Kyle and Madeleine, experienced challenges at birth. Kyle was born two months premature and had to undergo four surgeries during the first few years of his life. My brave little son went into cardiac arrest three times. Madeleine, too, had to undergo surgery at nine months old to correct a cleft palate, with ongoing issues that persisted after the surgery.

That both of my little ones were experiencing medical challenges, especially at such an early age, made it very, very difficult for me to go back to work after my maternity leave was over—a highly problematic prospect if you are the primary breadwinner, which I certainly was. And even if I could have afforded childcare, it would have needed to be highly specialized and, therefore, much too expensive. No one knew how to feed my little girl but me. How do you feed an infant who can't suck a bottle because she has a hole in her mouth? Fortunately, my mom came to help me out, which allowed me to go back to work, but even with her help, additional challenges kept coming down the conveyor belt.

As a Vice President at Netflix, international travel was a normal part of my not-so-normal life. Somehow, I got myself back in the saddle and managed, for the time being anyway, to juggle all of the balls. But it was becoming more and more of a struggle, particularly with the intense and constant travel.

Every second I spent with my children was sacred time—perfect, precious time—which made it more difficult for me to manage the moments that *weren't* sacred, and the moments spent flying from country to country, continent to continent. As much as I loved my job and everything it represented, I missed my babies, and my babies missed me. The stress of it all was becoming oppressive; it was wearing me down and wearing me out. And back then, in 2016, remote work was not yet a viable option for the masses, certainly not like it is today.

It was the stress, I thought, that was causing me to lose so much weight. I was turning forty, and I'd lost thirty pounds, even though I wasn't trying. I was feeling fatigued, uncomfortable, and out of sorts. I turned to my doctors for guidance, but they were confounded. "We need to run more tests," became the medical mantra to which I grew uncomfortably accustomed. Finally, after a full year of being poked, pricked, and prodded like a human cushion, and after being tested for endocrine issues, parasites, HIV, and just about every other malady under the sun, they found it.

They found the sarcoma.

Because I am such an eminently practical person who likes to solve a problem rather than cry over it, I felt relieved by the diagnosis. Now we could get on with the process of kicking this disease in its ass. Now we knew *precisely* what we were dealing with, the fight could begin. But in other ways, the diagnosis presented new problems. Chemotherapy and extensive international travel were not a good combination. In fact, for me, it could have proved a *lethal* combination. Even going into HQ was hazardous. Back then, if you had a cold or the sniffles, most people still went to work, but to be exposed to those germs was simply not an option for me, not with my system already so severely compromised by both the tumor and the chemotherapy.

All arrows pointed to the most logical (and life-saving) option—a direction that made my heart heavy. I had to disengage from Netflix for my own health and well-being, and for the health and well-being of my children. Remember that the possibility of remote work, at that time anyway, was just that: remote. No one was doing it with any regularity. So, although I needed to close the door on Netflix, another window of opportunity opened, as windows and doors often do when we least expect it.

Finally, I was back home with my babies. I was home, where those sacred moments with my children—those micro-moments and simple encounters I thought I'd lost forever—could unfold before me again. I was home, where *healing* could happen.

I knew that leaving Netflix was the right decision—although it wasn't a *decision* as much as it was a *necessity*, or maybe it was a decision born out of necessity. However, the words used to describe it aren't quite as important as the *emotions* that flowed from it. Even though I knew I'd made the right decision, I was suddenly vulnerable, uncertain of my future, and afraid. What would happen next? Where would I land? How would I fare physically? I was leaving my dream job, completely unsure of my next steps. What I *was* sure of, though, was that some of those steps had to include healing and spending time with my family. Working at Netflix was the best job I've ever had in my life, but here's the reality: I couldn't do it anymore. The two-part lesson here is realize when change must be made, then make it.

I didn't see my departure as a *defeat* as much as I saw it as a necessary mandate. And therein lies another lesson: know what your priorities are, and don't let anything (not even the best job you've ever had) stand in the way of meeting those priorities.

I realize now that, in a very real way, my illness was instrumental in opening a door that I never imagined existed. It was a door that would open to the rest of the world in a matter of a few short years, though nobody knew it yet, that led to new ways of working and transacting business successfully and efficiently that didn't include the traditional brick-and-mortar, everybody-gather-at-the-water-cooler model: the remote-working revolution.

Life on the Cutting Edge

Long before COVID-19 slammed into the world and forced all of us into new working and living patterns, some of us had already adopted the remote work model. Fortunately, the term "some of us" included me.

Shortly after leaving Netflix, I accepted a senior executive position at GitLab, the one DevOps platform that combines the ability to develop, secure, and operate software in a single application. This was (and is) cutting-edge stuff that allows us to work and live in the world in a completely different way, and the good news is that this position was completely remote. I couldn't have accepted it otherwise.

The other good news is that, even though I worked from home, I had employees in every corner of the globe who were also working remotely as well. When I first began at the company, we had employees in about forty different countries. Because it was so fast-growing, by the time I left the company, I had people in closer to sixty countries. This is where I learned about remote work. (There are so many rich lessons about remote work that I devote an entire chapter to it later in the book, so keep reading.)

GitLab was (and is) bold. Brave. Boundary-less. Completely virtual and unapologetically visionary. The company tag line is "Everyone Can Contribute," and they believed and lived that principle to the fullest. There was no brick-and-mortar headquarters. This was a company that helped the world jump onto the remote work bandwagon when the global pandemic made the transition unavoidable. I consider it a blessing and a privilege to have played even a small role in blazing that trail towards remote work long before that path was traveled by the millions (perhaps billions) of workers who would come to rely on it as heavily as we once relied on those moments of connection in breakrooms and cafeterias across the USA and beyond.

*

Let's start the dive with what I consider the most important lesson of all: believing in yourself. The upcoming chapter "Take a Chance" lays the foundation for every other lesson in the book. Taking a chance, not just on yourself but on the people who work with and for you, is everything. Why? Because if you don't believe in yourself and in the people who surround you, you are doing nothing to perpetuate a constant cycle of confidence. This cycle should never, ever lose its momentum, and leaders are responsible for making its movement continuous. We already know this, of course, but sometimes it helps to be reminded.

2

Take a Chance

BEING AN EFFECTIVE LEADER MEANS knowing when to look at projects, priorities, and people through a more expansive lens. Yes, it is fitting and strategically appropriate to focus on whatever challenge is before you with laser-like accuracy. As a leader myself, I *get* that. But we must also always be willing to look beyond what's in front of us so that we can see the larger picture, even if what we see requires us to change directions, shift gears, or course correct.

Originally, this chapter was titled "Take a Chance *on Yourself*," because I wanted to focus on the importance of being willing to take risks on yourself and to embrace the fact that *you are worthy* of risk-taking and boundary-breaking. But all my training and experience as a senior executive, businessowner, entrepreneur, and strategic consultant has forced me to look at this through a wider lens. I realize now that we, as leaders, must learn to take chances not just on ourselves but on others as well. Growth and professional development occur when we take chances on *each other*. So, I shortened the title to expand the concept that risk-taking involves more than just me and more than just you. It involves the people around us as well. Our focus should not just be on our individual pursuits; you and your team are in this together.

Leadership, therefore, is about so much more than believing in and having confidence in oneself (though that's certainly important, too). It's also about believing and having confidence in the people within your organization who look to you for leadership, motivation, and development. After all, doesn't effective leadership involve tapping into the talent within your organization that is as yet untapped? About seeing within your employees the promise and potential that they might not have even seen in *themselves* quite yet?

This means that we must be able to see more than what lies before us. We must be able to see the power and potential that's still dormant within those around us, waiting to be awakened. Then, as an important next step, we must be willing to provide the tools, the resources, and the mechanisms to hone that talent and develop the latent potential in a way that will promote individuals' growth and eventually bring benefit to the larger organization.

So, leaders, ask yourselves these questions:

1. Am I doing all I can to promote and facilitate the professional development of my employees?
2. What tools and mechanisms do I need to develop on my own, with my senior executive colleagues, or in collaboration with the trained HR managers within the company to better support my employees?

3. What decisions do I need to make and what risks do I need to take to ensure that growth and positive change are constantly unfolding around me?

Ask these questions of yourself, then actively seek the answers. Remember that this is a two-step process.

Risks Can Become Rewards

I want to jump back to "risk" for a moment because the word is often, frankly, misunderstood. As leaders, we are typically trained to avoid risk at all cost. Our brains are trained to see risk-taking as foolhardy, even irresponsible; as a result, we ascribe little or no value to the task of taking chances.

In fact, most organizations devote extraordinary amounts of time, talent, and resources to stay as far away from risk-taking as possible. Risk management and cost mitigation are often critical to the smooth running of corporate engines, certainly within many HR departments, anyway. But let's expand our vision for a minute, push past our own fears, and force ourselves to understand that risk-taking is what provides a platform for growth and advancement—not just from a financial and organizational perspective but also from a more holistic, human perspective as well. Risk, then, is necessary, and the *right* kind of risk-taking is even healthy.

Knowing when and how to take *calculated* risks can mean the difference between growth and stagnation (for companies and people), between pushing forward into new territory or standing still on soil that is no longer fertile. I must be open enough, confident enough, and secure enough in my own leadership abilities to identify in others what has not yet been seen by the world. Therefore, when I throw my support and faith behind that new employee who is showing a glimmer of promise and create new opportunities for that employee to stress-test that potential and lean into those untapped skills, I am taking a risk, certainly, but it is not a *random* risk. This requires the gift of discernment. Is there risk involved with every investment in talent? You bet there is. But if we don't take the chance, if we don't listen to and act upon our instincts and sometimes see beyond that which is before us, we might miss the opportunity.

I think back to the story I shared in the previous chapter of when the head of HR at Cisco, Kate DeCamp, asked me whether I'd ever consider an international assignment. By saying an immediate "yes," I took a chance on myself and stepped up to the plate when the opportunity presented itself. But it was a risky for *both* of us, really. What if I'd dropped the ball once I crossed the Atlantic? What if I missed the performance mark and ended putting the company at risk? My coming up short would have reflected poorly on Kate for having made a misguided decision, and it would have also proved to the world (the executives at Cisco who defined my "world" in my twenties) that I wasn't up to the task. What if I'd stumbled so badly that I couldn't recover? Fortunately, none of those scenarios occurred, and one reason was because, instead of asking, "What happens if she fails?" Kate asked more expansive questions: "What happens if she *doesn't* fail? What happens if she *makes* it? What happens if she moves to Europe and ends up leading Employee Relations for Europe, the Middle East, Africa, and about forty-six other countries where the company has employees?" This is the scenario that actually unfolded.

I've already mentioned that I still keep in contact with Kate to this day, and I mention it again here simply because I'm proud of the fact that we have maintained that connection. Here's the lesson: maintain your contacts, not just because they're useful contacts, but because these contacts often evolve into meaningful friendships, as is the case with Kate.

Kate recently reflected on our time together at Cisco and remembered it fondly. "You literally glowed with talent," she told me. "It was obvious. But then you also passed the tests we gave you, too. So, it's about seeing the shiny and sharp, but then testing for depth. The biggest talents grow and learn with each successive challenge." What Kate says about the importance of leaders appreciating the "shiny and sharp" attributes in their employees—those qualities that stand out for the world to see—reflects the concept I mentioned at the beginning of this chapter: leaders are trained to see the obvious, to see the qualities in our employees that shine and glisten. But another true test of leadership is being able to see *beyond* the gloss and look at the people in our organizations more closely—"testing for depth," as Kate describes it.

Kate took a calculated risk and it paid off. It paid off not just for me, as a young manager who'd been steered onto a path that ended up jettisoning my personal and professional growth, and not just for Kate, as a confident, courageous leader who believed in the promise and potential of new talent, but it also paid off for the organization by bringing value to its bottom line. Everyone benefitted. Everyone grew.

So, whether it's taking a chance on a new, unproven employee, or launching a new product, or starting an entirely new line of business, always try to embrace the concept of calculated risk as a necessary part of growth and change. This will require a new way of thinking about risk and a renewed effort to say "yes," instead of "no," but this broader perspective is realistic and attainable.

Taking a chance on someone else is risky business. But trust your instincts as a leader. And remember that from great risks can come great rewards. This was also evident to me as a senior executive at GitLab, where I was also able to see, firsthand, how jumping in with both feet, even though you don't yet know the water's depth, can bring untold success and create bold new frontiers, not just in the business world but in the real, everyday world we live in.

When I joined GitLab, a few other companies were using the remote work model, but not many. And there were even fewer using an *entirely* remote model like GitLab was. Today, of course, in this post-pandemic world, the workplace has been forever redefined, and remote work is realistic, attainable, and in many cases, the preferred mode of working; it now feels *familiar.* But ground-breaking, cutting-edge companies like GitLab are the ones who paved the way. The pandemic, as treacherous and destabilizing as it was, did not create the technical tsunami for GitLab that it created for most other organizations who didn't yet know how to adapt. When the pandemic hit, GitLab was ready for the onslaught because they'd already established working practices that ensured their resilience, their flexibility, and their adaptability. They'd already drawn for the world a perfect illustration of a business that believed in themselves enough to take a chance on doing things differently. Today, they are a public company, regarded by many (including me) as the standard-bearer for workplace innovation.

Prior to joining GitLab, I'd had zero experience working with remote teams. But I took a chance on a new area, a new company, and a new way of leading and living, and the risk has paid off in the form of personal growth and professional development that I never thought possible. Today, I'm seen as someone who can really help other companies navigate this world of workplace flexibility; it is what I know best—and I know it from a deeply personal perspective. When I joined GitLab, I immediately acquired staff and talent across the globe. With a single click, I had virtual access to extraordinary talent in nearly every part of the world. And we worked as a cohesive, collaborative team, even though we were as far apart geographically as humans can be. My experience at GitLab taught me that proximity has little to do with productivity. Indeed, if anything, remote work *done correctly* allows us to leapfrog over the traditional brick-and-mortar constraints of cramming everyone into the same office and presents new work possibilities that are seemingly limitless.

So, to GitLab, I express great gratitude for believing in themselves, for believing in their people, and for transforming something that was unseen by the wider world into something real and tangible, without borders or boundaries. In a very real way, they helped lay the foundation for other companies who would very suddenly, due to the pandemic, be forced to navigate the choppy, uncharted (for them) waters of remote work.

I was drawn to GitLab initially by a sense of necessity. I needed to stay home, and I also needed to work at the same time. GitLab provided this innovative option. But I was also drawn to the company because I believed in their mission; I believed in their bold vision. The founders and executives at GitLab took a chance on themselves, yes. But they also took a chance on every single person they hired, from every single corner of the world, and they also took a chance on *me*.

If that doesn't paint the picture of how a company can turn great risk into even greater reward, then I simply don't know what is.

Step onto the Stage

When we learn to take chances, whether it's taking a chance on ourselves or taking a chance on others, we force ourselves (in the most positive sense of the word) to get up on that stage and sing. I use the brave and purposeful act of stepping up onto the stage metaphorically, of course, but I have a literal example, too.

When I was about fifteen years old, I went with my parents on a family trip to Nashville, Tennessee. One night, we went to a well-known restaurant and bar called The Stagecoach, where patrons were occasionally invited onstage to sing along with the band. Imagine my horror, then, when a band member locked eyes with me and asked me to come up and sing with them. Had I ever done anything even remotely like that in the past? Did I have any formal training (or even informal, for that matter) as a singer? The answers: no and no. Did his unexpected invitation to get up there and sing stop me doing just that? Since you know me a little better by now, you might already know the answer to that question: I got up on that stage, regardless of the fear that was stirring in my heart. I didn't shy away from the guitar player standing on that stage, his arm outstretched towards me. The long and short of it was this: his invitation shocked me . . . but it didn't *stop* me. It didn't stop me from stepping up onto that stage and singing my heart out. Or at least trying to, anyway.

I'd never had the experience of singing in front of an audience, but I believed in myself enough to be able to get up there and give it a go. Keep in mind this wasn't karaoke, either. The lyrics weren't scrolling down a monitor in front of me. I was up there singing on my own, well, with a professional band. We were making our own music, and I was, for a moment anyway, a member of their group!

I know now that another important lesson about leadership was given to me in that moment: Step onto that stage—whatever "stage" it happens to be—when the opportunity presents itself and *do not wait to be asked twice*, because that second "ask" might never come.

I ended up singing two songs that night: Lorrie Morgan's "Out of Your Shoes," and the Judds' "Grandpa (Tell me 'Bout the Good Old Days)." After the first song, the guitarist leaned over and whispered to me, "You're doing good, but hold the mic a little closer to your mouth so we can *hear* you!" I didn't let the fact that I'd not used the mic correctly dampen my enthusiasm or my confidence. I simply adjusted. Course-corrected. Pulled the mic closer to my mouth and continued singing. And by the time I got to that second song, I was actually having a good time! Was it a Grammy-worthy performance? Of course not. Did the experience lead to singing stardom? Again, no. Those questions are irrelevant. The point is that the experience didn't *have* to lead to anything bigger for it to have been of value. It was valuable for what it was, and for what benefits it provided, which were:

1. Being one of the first opportunities in my young life to step onto a new stage (new to me) without fear of judgment.

2. Being a fine, fun, and enduring memory for my entire family that still makes all of us smile to this very day.

3. Showing my fifteen-year-old self she wasn't afraid to take a chance on herself, and that she didn't put limitations on herself that would stop her getting onto the stage, adjusting her mic, and singing her heart out with a group of professional musicians in Nashville, Tennessee.

The message to leaders is this: Sometimes it is necessary to step onto a new stage and out of your own comfort zone—not because you think it might lead to something great, but just for the sake of getting up there and *doing it*. In fact, as leaders, it's important to show our employees that we are not the experts in everything, that we don't know all there is to know, and that we ourselves are always growing, always evolving. This not only helps our employees understand us better as human beings, it also shows them that *all* of us are constantly learning. Constantly changing. Constantly taking chances on ourselves in ways that ensure our continued growth and development.

So, go ahead. Get up there on a new stage, on whatever stage is before you, and *sing*, only if you're up there for a few minutes. Heck, even try to muster enough self-confidence and courage to be able to make an absolute fool of yourself every now and then, even if it's only for a minute. It's probably best for everyone involved if the making-a-fool-of-yourself part is, indeed, short-lived, but showing that kind of openness and vulnerability is itself a show of strength and will lead to great growth.

Whatever you do, just don't stay stuck on doing what you do best, even though that's the natural (and safest) inclination. Continuing to do what you do best doesn't necessarily make you better or stronger or faster; it can actually become stultifying and leave you in a leadership rut—and you owe yourself more than that. Even more importantly, you owe your team and your employees more than that, too.

Additionally, entrepreneurs and young executives still fairly new to the leadership game should remember this: You'll never get good at new things, never develop new strategies, products, or potential new lines of business, unless you teach yourself to take chances. *So, strengthen this skill at every turn, rather than avoid it at any cost*. It will be good for your employees. It will be good for your organization. It will be good for your overall character (which we will discuss in more detail later in the book).

Create new opportunities. Promote new ways of being and doing. Lead the way towards new ways of leading. Get out your hammer and nails and begin constructing new stages to step onto, not just for yourself but for those who are looking to you for leadership, for development, and for growth. And when you step onto your new stage, *do NOT do what you've always done best, but what you've never done before.* Step onto that new stage and sing a new song.

Trust me when I tell you that you'll be happy you did.

Bollywood or Baseball: Take a Chance on It All!

Netflix is a perfect example of an organization that not only encourages its executives to step out of their own comfort zones but also *requires* them to make those leaps and take those steps as a necessary form of growth and development.

The company's executive off-site meetings were always carefully designed and purposefully orchestrated, and we had them regularly. The idea was to bring together the senior executives on a regular basis to engage in spontaneous team-building exercises that would create a sense of closeness and collaboration.

Some of these forums were highly creative, "make-a-fool-of-yourself-for-a-minute" activities, where participants were forced to step outside their comfort zone. Yes, the company had a strategic purpose in mind when hosting these off-sites, but maybe here's the most important purpose of all: these off-sites were just good old-fashioned *fun*. During one executive off-site in Germany, for example, we had to break up into small groups to sing karaoke. My group (which happened to include then-CEO Reed Hastings) decided to rewrite the lyrics of our song altogether: tradition be damned! We had a great time stepping outside of our "zone" to create harmony that we otherwise would never have made.

During that executive off-site, I drew from my onstage-with-the-band experience in Nashville, as a fifteen-year-old girl. In fact, it was because I took a chance on myself way back then that I was able to stand on that stage with my Netflix colleagues and feel even more comfortable and confident about taking a chance with them. History does, indeed, repeat itself. It's our responsibility as leaders to learn from history and apply its lessons.

During another executive off-site in India, we did Bollywood dancing. Yes, there were moments of sheer terror at these off-sites, and yes, we exposed the more vulnerable sides of ourselves by trying something new (usually before vast audiences, no less), but by coming together and taking the collective plunge, we all grew. We all expanded. We all learned the value of risk-taking and collaboration, and we all learned to trust each other more. We were all reminded that work and hanging with your colleagues can also be *fun*; it need not be drudgery. Most importantly, we all learned the importance of taking a chance—not just on ourselves, but on each other.

The last executive off-site I attended before I left Netflix took place in Cuba, where, as was fitting and appropriate, the planned group activity was baseball. Obviously, each team wanted to win, but victory for the sake of victory wasn't the be-all, end-all goal. What was important was that each team came together to work as one. To take a chance on each other. To discover our strengths and weaknesses and make those strengths and weaknesses work for us in a way that can only be discovered and revealed by being in a group dynamic like that.

In all the off-sites, we came together, with all of our flaws and foibles, eager to grow, ready to win, but also willing to take a chance on each other. Those off-sites also helped keep us humble.

They helped remind us that we are humans first, and leaders second. The best way to put it is like this: We are *human leaders who must rely on each other for growth, advancement, and expansion.* And we were human leaders who were simply having a bunch of fun—even if we didn't sing well, couldn't dance, or couldn't hit a baseball!

I look back on it now and reflect on how my own life and the leadership lessons I've learned over the years keep overlapping. I remember standing on that softball field as a young employee in my twenties, when I was at Cisco, and how one person at that game who was willing to take a calculated chance on me (Kate DeCamp) set me on the trajectory of my career.

I think about my willingness to take a chance on myself back then, too, which in a very real way, eventually guided me to *another* baseball field, this time in Cuba, no longer in my twenties but in my forties, playing baseball with some of the most brilliant, creative minds in the world—my Netflix colleagues—as the citizens of Cuba watched us play from the stands. I think about how *none* of this would have happened at all had I not been willing to take the chance on myself. I reflect on how fortunate I am to have learned, as a leader, that it's not just about taking a chance on yourself; it's about taking a chance on others as well.

Stop a minute now to give this some personal reflection. Take yourself back to when you were new to the working world and might not have even recognized your own potential just yet. Was there a teacher, during your early school days, who made a difference to your life's trajectory? Maybe a mentor who took the time and made the effort to show you that they saw something in you that you didn't yet even see in yourself? Think about the person who took a chance on you and who taught you the importance of taking a chance on yourself.

Equally important, ask yourself these questions, too:

1. Are you playing that role in someone else's life today?
2. Are you bold enough, confident enough, discerning enough in your leadership abilities, to take a chance on others in a way that will ensure their continued growth and development?
3. Can you change your relationship with the concept of risk? Retrain your brain to embrace calculated risk as a necessary part of growth? Look at the world through a more expansive lens?

You don't have to have all the answers yet. You just need to be willing to engage in the search for them.

3

Try or Die:
Cultivating Tenacity

I'M GOING TO OPEN THIS chapter with a concept I touched
on in the previous chapter: we are humans first and leaders
second. As humans who happen to also be leaders, we are an
extraordinary kaleidoscope of various traits and characteristics.
There is no single make or model. This is why I cannot write a
book about leadership that is surgically precise and perfectly
regimented. I suppose I *could*, but I wouldn't want to, nor do I
intend to, because the principles of leadership must in some way
mirror the varied and diverse humans that we are.

Any book on leadership should account for—indeed, cele-
brate—our strengths and weaknesses, our capabilities and vul-
nerabilities. We are not automatons. The challenges we face as
leaders are as multi-layered as the humans we are and who
surround us. This stuff can't always fit into neat boxes, nor should

we try to force a fit. That's not what leadership is about. Leadership doesn't lend itself to strict regimentation. Instead, you'll see some similarities and parallels between many of these leadership principles and characteristics that I present. There will be some necessary "spillage," if you will, from chapter to chapter, simply because many of these essential qualities of leadership are so closely aligned and related. Yes, there will be a bit of overlap, because that's what humans do sometimes: we overlap. I don't see this as a bad thing at all; I see it as an acknowledgment that leadership is *alive*—and it lives because *we* are alive.

However, while there are no rigid, compartmentalized boxes that we should try to force ourselves to fit into, there *are* common characteristics and traits we can aspire to attain that will make us better: stronger, more efficient, more impactful. I suppose the best way to put it is like this: While you have your own leadership style and I have mine, we both stand under the same leadership umbrella, together. Certain characteristics, traits, and principles are commonly held by the most effective leaders; these are *uniform* traits, yet they can still be freely and creatively expressed by each individual leader.

Under this leadership umbrella, then, are the essential characteristics that comprise leadership at its best, and those of us who stand under this umbrella together will remain dry during the storm (or at least not soaked). This is a comforting assurance since we all know that storms, tsunamis, and setbacks are inevitable. As we stand together underneath the common shelter, will are bound to find, again and again, comfortable conceptual overlaps. They are necessary and inevitable. In the previous chapter, for example, the importance of our learning to take a chance on ourselves and our employees requires many of the same leadership skills that we examine in this chapter about never giving up, yet they are still two separate and distinct threads. The point is this: Even though these are two threads, when these two leadership characteristics are bound and twisted *together*, they create a stronger and more resilient rope to which we can all cling as we figure out how best to lead most effectively. Don't all of us have a responsibility to pull together as many of these principles as we possibly can?

When it comes to leading with confidence, with integrity, with humility, and with courage, *we must never give up*. In fact, this is a perfect example of a leadership principle that can (and does) spill over quite comfortably into just about every chapter in this book. Overlaps abound.

Let's do a deeper dive now and look at what it *looks like* to never give up. Whether we're talking about leading others or living life itself, being able to call on an inner strength and an unwavering tenacity is essential . . . especially when the going gets rough.

A Matter of Life and Death

When I first received my sarcoma diagnosis, the picture looked grim. The doctors told me that in order to fight it effectively and get rid of the rare tumor growing inside my body, extreme measures would be required. They'd need to remove between four to six ribs from my left chest wall, where the tumor was located. After the ribs had been removed, they'd need to relocate all the tissue and veins from the back of my chest to the front and come in with what they described as "fake skin"—a Kevlar-like material that would cover my heart and lungs. They also predicted that I'd most probably have to stay on chemo for the rest of my life.

This was not an option I was willing to accept lightly. It certainly was not how I wanted to live out the rest of my life. After hearing the diagnosis and the prognosis, though, I realized something crucial: Just because this radical plan of attack had been presented to me as the next logical step, that didn't mean I had to *accept* it as the next logical step! It was my life, after all. There is an important leadership message here: Do not always follow the path of least resistance. If you believe in something strongly enough (in my case, the continuation and quality of my *life*), then you must never give up or be satisfied with accepting what is presented to you simply because it's presented as the best (or only) way to proceed.

> Beware of the status quo. It is overrated. Don't always seek "safe" harbor because—news flash!—it is not always the safest place to be.

Keep in mind that my life, at that time, had become a swirling vortex of sorts. Lots was happening, some good things, some not so good . . . actually, some downright crappy things. Not only was I faced with this sudden and severe diagnosis, I was also going through a difficult divorce, still navigating the joys (and challenges) of mothering two small children, and holding down a very demanding-but-rewarding job as a senior executive at Netflix. All of this, combined with possibility (no, make that the *probability*) that I would be leaving my two small children motherless and my new fiancé without his "other half" could have been enough to overwhelm me, if it hadn't been for these two immutable facts: I am not easily overwhelmed and, second, I do not easily give up.

Those two facts automatically led me to three stark realities:

1. I was definitely not ready or willing to endure a lifetime of chemo.
2. I was definitely not ready to die.
3. Not only was I not ready to die, I was thirsty to keep living.

This third reality is a mantra that follows me around and often echoes through my thoughts: the goal is to thrive, not just survive. Those were just the numbers I needed to continue fighting my fight, and those were just the numbers I needed to help me make the decision to kick this illness directly in its ugly ass.

I need to add an important side note at this point: I do not wish to paint a portrait of myself as Superwoman here, nor do I wish to appear insensitive to those who have faced similar or far worse battles but have made different choices than the choices I made. My heart goes out to those who didn't win the battle, who didn't have an option, like I did, to beat back their illness. I hold those who are forced to deal with serious illnesses of any kind in the highest respect, regardless of *how* they choose to fight their battles. It all comes down to personal choice and available options. And to all who have struggled or are struggling today with far more serious illnesses than mine, I hold you in the highest honor and esteem, and I share my empathy and support.

But back to the rising-sun revelation I had when I was diagnosed. Once I decided to reject that extreme course of action, that was that, and I sought a second opinion. I searched for and found an alternative that felt far more palatable to me. Was it risky? Extremely. In fact, my new medical team at Sloane Kettering was across the country, which definitely made for an arduous (and costly) commute to receive ongoing treatment, but it was well worth the effort.

The fact that I am alive today, strong and healthy, is proof positive that it was worth the effort. I need to write that sentence again in a different way and, heck, maybe even shout it from the nearest rooftop, just because it feels so good to shout about and write these very words: *Because I did not give up then, I am alive today.*

The risky treatment I decided upon was both "new" and "alternative." It was considered a fairly unorthodox procedure by most of the medical community and no one else was performing this surgery with any regularity. In fact, I was one of the first few patients to have undergone this procedure to treat my particular type of sarcoma, which made me feel like a pioneer of sorts—a humble and very grateful pioneer—given that I was quite literally putting my life in the hands of those brilliant surgeons and practitioners who were paving new paths in medical science . . . and saving my life to boot.

The procedure I underwent was called *cryoablation,* a much more readily accepted and practiced in medicine today but not on many practitioners' radar screens at the time. Cryoablation is a procedure that uses extreme cold to destroy diseased tissue. Long, hollow needles called "cryoprobes" were inserted into my chest where the tumor was located. The probes were filled with a potent fluid that would attack and kill the tumor by freezing it. But all this killing came with a price. The fluid would also kill some of the healthy nerves, tissue, and bones in close proximity to the tumor, which would also mean, as it was explained to me, that some of my bones (especially my ribs) would "die."

Even though the surgery was highly successful, thank goodness, I still deal with some of the fallout today. My lungs, for example, do not function at full capacity, and the lobe of my left lung remains damaged and somewhat compromised from the procedure. And the ribs that were affected by the procedure are referred to as "dead ribs," which means they are extremely weak and brittle. One time, in the middle of getting a massage, I remember hearing a loud crack. This was the sound, as you might have guessed, of one of my ribs breaking. They were so weakened by the surgery that they simply could not withstand the pressure of the massage.

The silver lining—and there's always a silver lining, as you've heard me say before—is that because the rib was already considered "dead," the fracture caused me virtually no pain or discomfort. In fact, only the audible cracking told me it had fractured. I still remember as if it happened yesterday, the *pop* and then the *crack* of my rib giving way. I can still feel the bone splintering inside me. In fact, the very memory of that sound serves as a stark reminder that I had, indeed, *been broken* to a degree both figuratively and literally. A part of me had been weakened. A part of me had succumbed to the pressure and simply snapped.

The memory of that sound also serves to make me feel more *human*, really, because it leads me to these questions that I will ask you to contemplate for yourself, as a leader and as a human who lives in this world amongst other humans: Aren't *all* of us broken in some way? Aren't all of us vulnerable, exposed, and/or frightened of *something* in our lives? And doesn't this acknowledgment and acceptance make us stronger leaders and more multi-dimensional humans? Why should we be afraid of or embarrassed about embracing our brokenness and accepting the areas within us that simply aren't built to withstand the additional pressure?

As leaders, we must be willing to show vulnerability, too. And we must be willing to allow our employees the necessary luxury of sharing their own vulnerabilities and weaknesses as well, without fear of judgment or retribution. This means creating safe space within your organization that allows room for sharing, for open communication, and for honest, transparent dialogue.

Throughout my ordeal, I was insecure, uncertain, and I confess, absolutely terrified of the prospect of leaving my children motherless, but *I never gave up*. I also developed tools and techniques to make it through the storm. This is also what we must do as leaders: develop tools that we *share* with others, because when it comes down to it, we're all standing under the same leadership umbrella, hoping for motivation and help.

My "Beat Desi" Playlist

Here, I want to share a tool that helped lead me through that storm.

I named my illness "Desi" because I strongly believe that when we name our enemies, we are better able to beat them back. If you recall from the Introduction, my tumor was the "Desmoid" tumor, so you understand why I named this enemy "Desi." There was definitely a method to my madness. But more than madness, there was all this *music*.

Music has always fueled my soul and soothed my spirit. Take a listen to some of the songs listed below that filled me with renewed energy and fierce determination as I was fighting the fight of my life. I lost myself in this music day and night, during my best moments and my worst. And I didn't just sing these songs while I was sick. I *screamed* them when I had to. I cried them. I roared them. And I shared them with others who were suffering. I gave the list to a friend of mine who was suffering from breast cancer, and she told me it helped get her through. And now, I share the list with you.

If you're facing what seems like an insurmountable challenge, remember that giving up is not an option. Let this music and these songs be your fuel, or create your own playlist. Take hold of the challenge that is before you and don't let go. And above all, never, ever, ever give up.

"FIGHT LIKE A GIRL"	BOMSHEL
"BEAT IT"	MICHAEL JACKSON
"HOMECOMING QUEEN"	KACEY MUSGRAVES
"I'M GONNA LOVE YOU THROUGH IT"	MARTINA MCBRIDE
"THIS ONE'S FOR THE GIRLS"	MARTINA MCBRIDE
"IF YOU'RE GOING THROUGH HELL"	RODNEY ATKINS
"CRY PRETTY"	CARRIE UNDERWOOD
"I DIDN'T KNOW MY OWN STRENGTH"	WHITNEY HOUSTON
"I WON'T BACK DOWN"	TOM PETTY
"I WILL SURVIVE"	GLORIA GAYNOR
"WE ARE THE CHAMPIONS"	QUEEN
"WHATEVER IT TAKES"	IMAGINE DRAGONS

*

Variations of "Giving Up"

When we look at essential leadership qualities, especially that of cultivating our tenacity (i.e., strengthening our inner resolve, and remaining firmly rooted in our refusal to give up or walk away), we need to look at all the gray areas and hidden layers within this principle as well.

Let's return to the concept I keep swinging back to, which is becoming my mantra of sorts, because it bears repeating here, particularly in the context of never giving up: we are humans first and leaders second. That is to say we are *human leaders* who bring to each situation and every challenge a certain amount of overlap, imprecision, and even messiness. There will always be gray areas and variations. It is the nature of the human condition. For instance, there's a difference between giving up and, say, learning from your mistakes and deciding that moving on is the most prudent course of action. Don't get them confused. If, for example, a young manager continually slips off the rails or goes against the grain or culture of the organization in a way that is detrimental, then I am not "giving up" on that employee if I change his or her trajectory. I am simply directing them towards other options that will be better suited for his or her talent and temperament. As a leader, that is my responsibility. I don't see this as "giving up" on that employee at all. Indeed, by exploring what other options might work best for everyone involved and redirecting their path towards a more productive outcome, I am affording that employee an opportunity to change, to grow, and, hopefully, to flourish, either in another capacity within the organization or outside of the organization altogether.

Knowing when to redirect and course-correct isn't giving up. It's demonstrating resilience, flexibility, and *discernment.* Of course, these leadership skills will strengthen within you over time, since the skills deepen and evolve as we ourselves deepen and evolve as humans. This is an important lesson to impart to new managers and those at the beginning of their leadership journey: we get better in due course.

Also remember this simple, unavoidable truth: setbacks are inevitable, both in leadership and in life.

You cannot let these setbacks derail you. Nor can you stand so long within a crisis that it blows you (and/or your company) so far off track that recovery becomes impossible. You must learn from your mistakes, allow yourself to be strengthened, rather than weakened, by your setbacks, and be *decisive* about whether to walk away or remain in the midst of the mistakes and try to solve them. Staying stuck, however, is not an option.

I offer up Netflix yet again as a shining example of a company that wasn't afraid to take a chance, or hesitant to shift gears and course-correct to allow the organization to rebound in ways rarely witnessed by the business world before. You'll no doubt remember when Netflix decided to spin off its DVD unit into a new company called Qwikster, and how the decision was met with immediate opposition by subscribers who weren't willing to pay an increased fee. The company lost around 800,000 customers as a result. Was this a setback? Of course. But did the company let this setback derail them? Of course not. Derailment was not an option. Instead, Netflix apologized to customers (then-CEO Reed Hastings even issued a direct apology to subscribers for the "lack of respect and humility" the company showed in coming to and communicating the decision), and the plan was quickly abandoned. The company had enough courage to try something new, and when they realized it wasn't working, they didn't give up ... they listened to subscribers and made an informed decision to switch gears. Customers spoke, Netflix listened, and out of that dynamic came incredible benefit—as painful as it was getting there. In fact, Netflix split the company internally to let Qwikster survive to become an amazing logistics company, unburdened by the Netflix brand. I believe history shows Reed made the right decision, in the end.

Not only did Netflix rebound with extraordinary grace and rapidity, but its stock went on to become the amongst the most valuable currency in the world. The company learned from its mistakes, took quick, corrective action, and proceeded from a place of humility and grace. This is what world-class companies do. They not only learn from their missteps, they grow from them, too.

Lessons from the Cockpit

As I am writing this book, I am also studying to become a licensed pilot. I've always been attracted to both the freedom and the precision of flying; I like that those two opposing forces—freedom and precision—coexist when you're flying thousands of feet up. (And, I admit, the prospect of piling my family and four dogs into a plane and heading wherever the heck we want definitely holds a certain appeal, too.)

Recently, as I was studying one of the FAA manuals, the stark similarities between flying and leading really jumped out at me. Interestingly, the manual listed the primary reason for mishaps and accidents during flight not as equipment failure or mechanical breakdown, as one might guess, but *human error*.

This unexpected emphasis on the human equation surprised me, particularly coming from a document as precise, as finite, and as formulaic as an FAA manual. If something goes wrong mid-flight, for instance, the quickest way to go from bad to worse, as the manual explains, is for the pilot to experience a loss of confidence or to be overcome by feelings of helplessness and inevitability. When human emotions like this take over—especially in the cockpit—things will spiral downward very quickly (literally). This is why preparation, preparation, and more preparation— as well as checking, cross-checking and triple-checking—are all-important to any pilot. This kind of exhaustive, relentless preparation is what builds confidence, and confidence is what builds resilience and tenacity, particularly in the face of crisis.

There's another side to that coin, too. Just as lack of confidence is dangerous to a pilot, so also is *over*confidence. A pilot who feels that nothing can go wrong is a pilot who might make careless mistakes and missteps. Either extreme can compromise a pilot's judgment and, hence, their ability to properly and responsibly react during a crisis. Balance is key.

Don't these same principles apply to *all* of us, as leaders, too? When the going gets rough, when unexpected turbulence tosses us (and our crew and passengers) this way and that, it is not an option for the pilot to simply throw in the towel and walk away. Giving up is not feasible. Just as the passengers and flight crew depend on their pilot to fly them through the turbulence, our employees, clients, customers, and the communities we serve rely upon us. The silver lining here (a theme that's becoming more prominent as we go deeper into the book) is that confidence has a way of growing stronger and deeper over time. The more experience a leader has, the more discerning and confident they will become as they continue forward in their career. Similarly, the more miles a pilot flies, the more hours they accumulate in their logbook, the more confident they will become when those dark storm clouds descend, and the resulting turbulence becomes potentially destabilizing. The *human qualities* of being both a leader and a pilot are what will spell the difference between a safe landing and aborted takeoff. We are humans first . . . even the FAA says so!

There are many lessons within this chapter, then, that pertain to both leadership and life: lessons that teach us the difference between giving up and walking away; lessons that remind us that we are all standing under the same leadership umbrella, doing what we can to offer the best of ourselves to each other, our employees, our organizations, and, ultimately, the larger world; lessons about life and death, even; lessons about how standing up to the status quo is sometimes the only thing that will save us; and lessons, really, about the joy that comes from being able to fly through the turbulence with confidence, courage, and unyielding tenacity.

After all, effective leadership means pulling out of the gate, taxiing down the runway, and taking off into the clear blue skies. Then, when the storms come—and they *will* come—being able to draw on our skills in a way that keeps us cool, calm, and confident . . . not just in the cockpit, but in life and leadership as well.

4

Survival of
the Fittest

THE CULTURE OF ANY ORGANIZATION, large or small,
is a living, breathing thing. It has a pulse. A heartbeat. A voice.
An appetite. And like any living thing, if you don't feed it, it will
either wither and die or become a monster.

This concept is important to understand and embrace, espe-
cially when we look at leadership and organizational culture
through the prism of *change*. Why? Because if leaders don't
learn to accept change as a necessary nutrient and vital part of
any well-balanced organizational "diet," they are contributing
to the malnourishment—and, oftentimes, starvation—of that
organization.

If you, as a leader, aren't doing everything within your power
to ensure your organizational culture welcomes and invites
change, even when that change might feel uncomfortable, how

can you expect your company and your employees to flourish? To become more resilient? To push into new spaces and explore previously unexplored territory? To build up enough muscle mass to stand strong against crisis and chaos when they arrive (as we know they inevitably will)?

This chapter will help us discover how we, as leaders, can learn not just to adapt and survive through change but also thrive in its midst. We'll also examine the importance of being brave enough, bold enough, and confident enough in ourselves, our talent, and our resources to *create* change. It's one thing to passively accept change, but to actively "go after it" requires a different skillset and mental framework altogether. We can train our brains and encourage our employees to be both passive and active with regard to change.

Look at it like this: Unless we've been fed a steady, nutrient-rich diet on a continuous basis (not just on a quarterly or annual basis), we will not be able to stand up to the rigors and the intensity of the coming storms. We will not be able to *absorb* change as efficiently and strategically if we have not embraced change as a normal part of living, working, and being. When that strong wind slams into us with hurricane-force intensity, be it a pandemic or product failure, we do not have to be uprooted. We can learn to lean into the wind without being swept away by it. We can learn to redistribute the weight of its impact by adopting—and then adapting—new ways of thinking and thriving that were once unimaginable.

If you want to compete boldly, to flourish fully, and to evolve responsibly in this rapidly evolving world, embracing change is the only choice. Let me put it another way:

> We must change our relationship with change.

This won't happen overnight, nor will it happen by itself or on its own. Hard work is involved, not just in relation to our actions but also in our overall philosophical approach to change itself that requires a purposeful expansion of our leadership mindset. Before we can change our behavior, we must change our thinking; we start on the inside and work our way out. First and foremost should come the recognition that change is not the enemy; it is a constant.

Evolution Is Inevitable

If we look at change not as a threat, a setback, or indication of abject (or even implied) failure on our part, but rather as an inevitability, our shift in mindset can begin. The world is a radically different place than it was, say, five years ago; it's a radically different place than it was even 365 days ago; we have all felt the alteration, throughout the spectrum of business and at every level of daily life. The world has been both ravaged and propelled by change.

The questions you must ask yourself now are: Have *you* changed and adapted as the world around you has changed? And have you been able to feed your organization a steady, nutrient-rich diet that ensures its continued flexibility, adaptability, and resilience? If the answer to either (or both) of these questions is "no," do not despair. The simple recognition that you might need to put in a little more work to become more adaptable and resilient during these tumultuous times has already moved you a step in the right direction. Awareness must come before action.

When we become more vitally aware of the fact that evolution is inevitable, it forces our hand, in a sense, to evaluate how we want to respond to the changing world around us. Standing still, conducting "business as usual," remaining inert and disengaged, hunkering down, lying low and praying that the storm will pass are no longer viable options ... not when everyone around us is retooling, redefining, and reimagining themselves so they can stay in the game.

We've got to look at this through a wider lens. Once we expand our leadership vision and begin to look at change as an inevitable and constant process—a *necessary* process that facilitates growth—change itself can be seen as part of the solution that moves us forward, rather than a problem we must avoid at all costs. Strategies, policies, practices, and people are *meant* to evolve. Think of where the world would be if they hadn't! This mindset requires leaders to adapt a higher order of thinking. It requires us to "muscle up" and lean into the wind in a way that allows us to take our rightful place on this fast-moving evolutionary scale.

Change, then, is evolution, and evolution, by definition, is adaptation. Here's the bottom line: none of this is optional. The process is going to continually unfold around you, whether you buy into it or not, and so you might as well build it into development strategies. The question now becomes, "Why would you *not* want to become more adaptive, more resilient, and more courageous when it comes to embracing (and sometimes even initiating) change within your organization?"

We have all lived through a catastrophic event—the coronavirus pandemic. Its sudden arrival shifted the world on its axis, changing the way we worked, the way we lived, the way we interacted with each other, and most certainly the way we conducted business. But I don't believe it changed us as much it *should* have. What I mean is that many companies, for any number of reasons, were simply not able to respond to this global crisis as quickly or effectively as the situation demanded. The storm arrived too suddenly, and the winds were too strong and lasted too long. Adaptation, for many companies, was impossible. And as the crisis persisted, these were the companies that also struggled with organizational issues like reduced employee engagement and retention.

But during the pandemic, those companies that *did* create new models of leadership and new ways of adapting thrived. The companies that knew how to pivot, retool, and do things differently, who embraced the crisis because they *had* to if they wanted to survive, were the companies that ultimately made it through the storm. They searched for and found adaptive tools and techniques that made it possible for them to survive. Many of these companies, because they were able to improve their relationship with change, are now seeing higher retention rates, greater workforce engagement, and stronger balance sheets.

Leaders, understand this: the world will continue to evolve. Viruses will continue to mutate. Catastrophes will continue to unfold. Change will continue to occur. *Everything* evolves— groups, organizations, individuals—and if you don't become more adaptable, if you don't train your brain to respond to this evolutionary process more creatively and responsibly, you can be sure that the people around you who are willing and able to adapt (i.e., your competitors) will be the ones who will continue to win.

Evolution and change will occur with or without you; the process is inevitable. It exists independently of you and your leadership preferences. The question is whether or not you want to join the journey; whether you want to step onto the evolutionary escalator with confidence and grace.

I want to extend this invitation to you now: Step on. Join us. Bring your team with you.

There's enough room for all of us.

Go Where No One Has Gone Before

Embracing change doesn't just mean *responding* to change; let's expand our understanding a little more. Embracing change often means creating change. Forcing its hand. Breaking new ground by stepping into a bold, new space that has never been stepped into before, by anyone. This is when we actually *facilitate* the evolutionary process. This takes extraordinary vision, courage, creativity, resources, talent, and a leadership mindset that sees change as a necessary part of discovery, growth, and exploration.

Being a part of the executive leadership team at Netflix helped open my eyes to the fact evolution doesn't necessarily happen independently of us. It doesn't have to unfold only when the universe demands that it unfolds. Not at all. Evolution can also unfold when we *want* it to. Through our own actions and by virtue of our own sheer will, we can help the evolutionary process along! Pretty heady stuff, when you really think about it.

In this regard, I think of the time Netflix made the gargantuan leap from being a company that used traditional databases, like Oracle, to a company that moved to the cloud, which was groundbreaking, really, given that almost no other companies were using cloud services with any measurable consistency. Stepping into this new territory meant that our entire data team had to reskill and refocus in a way they'd never had to before. Was it risky? Of course it was, because we were *forcing* change, not just facing it.

By looking ahead and by adopting a higher level of thinking (the Netflix leadership saw change coming), they could see that fully embracing this new technology would allow work to be done in a way that it had never been done before. In doing so, the company paved the way for other businesses and industries to follow suit...which is precisely what happened. It broke the mold and set the standard. By moving billing and payments entirely to the cloud, Netflix not only gave its customers a new, more efficient way of doing business, it also paved the way for other companies (even its competitors) to follow suit, thus beginning the stampede towards cloud-based technology on a massive scale.

Netflix also hastened its own evolutionary growth, when it made the decision to move from mail-order DVD rental (their original focus) to streaming content, and then from streaming content to also creating content. I think I will describe this as a *purposeful evolution*.

It is this "purposeful evolution" mindset that has made Netflix stock one of the most valuable currencies in the world today. It is what moved the company from being an amazing logistics company, shipping out DVDs, to being a world-class hybrid company, both in entertainment and technology, born out of visionary leadership, amazing talent, and an audacious desire to go where no one else has ever gone before.

When it comes to change, therefore, the leadership team at Netflix has shown the rest of the business world that the art of building a company that is okay with change is making change okay. Period. No, this doesn't mean that mistakes won't happen. They will. But even when you fail, you learn. Obviously, it is best to avoid making catastrophic missteps (and if that's not possible, at least avoid repeating them), but we, as leaders, must give our people and ourselves the freedom to fail, the space to regroup, and the courage to create change rather than just react to it.

This is the most excellent way to evolve, don't you think?

Principles in Practice

It is one thing to preach the lofty principles of change and to stand on high extolling the philosophical virtues of evolutionary growth. It is another thing entirely to walk the walk. Unfortunately, there are too many leaders who talk a good game about the importance of change but never actually embrace it on any meaningful or sustainable level. Practicing what you preach is essential.

This is why I want to break this subject down to its grittiest level in a way that allows to us to look at evolution through the most fundamental lens of all: that of human existence; life as we live it every day, as normal, curious, vulnerable human beings who are simply trying to make it from one day to the next in the most meaningful and responsible way we can.

I have learned through experience that change is the only constant and that it is up to me, and only me, to be the person I aspire to be, the mother and wife I aspire to be, the leader, the mentor, the friend, the ... well, the list goes on and on. I know I must embrace and facilitate my own evolution whenever possible; I refuse to sit and wait for the universe to do it for me. And I must practice these evolutionary principles from a place of inner truth and authentic experience. I must create the change I want to see in myself.

Does this mean that the changes I've made in my own life haven't been scary? That they haven't often left me feeling vulnerable, uncertain, and anxious about what will come next? In most cases, before I've made a big change, I've felt all of the above. I am human, not Superwoman—and I say this *loudly*, as a proud declaration rather than apologetic admission. This declaration of imperfection and vulnerability doesn't minimize my strengths in any way. If anything, it *maximizes* my ability to stand up to (or walk away from) situations that are or will become harmful or destructive.

Yes, change, for me, is sometimes scary, but my ability to drive this change myself (whenever possible) makes it a little less frightening. Creating change in my own life affords me a measure of control. Whatever happens after I've set that change in motion is not always within my control, but I am okay with that because I know, no matter how it turns out, *it's gonna be okay in the end.* I suppose you could describe this as having faith, not just in myself or the future but faith in the immutable fact that even the messiest, most wrinkled situations have a way of eventually smoothing themselves out over time. It takes energy and purposeful effort too, of course, because what good is faith without action? But all of this, taken together, is what stands at the solid center of my relationship with change. I believe in myself, and I believe in my ability to facilitate change in a way that will protect me, nourish me, and facilitate my growth as a human being. The decision to change is not always easy, as we all know, but I have become very good at identifying my own voice . . . and when it speaks to me, I listen.

I use my first marriage, which ended in divorce, as an example. Was it a difficult decision to walk away from a person with whom I'd spent so many years, built a home, and formed a family? Someone with whom I established the predictable (and withstood the unpredictable) rhythms of life? Of course it was a difficult decision! But because it was also a *necessary* decision, the degree of difficulty became far more manageable.

I don't see my divorce as a failure, either. I see it as an affirmation that life itself changes over time, people grow apart, priorities change, difficulties arise that are sometimes insurmountable, and, out of all that, comes the stark awareness that change itself, in certain situations, *must be the mandate*. This mandate didn't make the decision any less frightening, but it did add clarity and confidence to my decision.

When I walked away, I didn't even really know what I was walking towards, since none of us know what the future holds, which was a little scary. All I knew was that I was becoming a single mother to two very young children. This was also around the same time I was diagnosed with the sarcoma—a sudden and potentially catastrophic change over which I had no control. My illness, as I've already mentioned in earlier chapters, also put into motion another unavoidable change, which was having to leave Netflix, which cut me to my core because it was the most extraordinary job I've ever had in my life. Yet, the change was necessary, so I made it.

My point here is that major changes were unfolding around me, some of my choosing, others not. Yet I kept living because *stopping* living was not an option in my mind. I kept pushing forward because standing still or ignoring the need for these changes were not options, either. In each and every case, I didn't have the luxury of thinking, "I'll just take a year or two to think about how I'm going to handle this." Rather, I stepped onto that evolutionary escalator and propelled myself towards change. It's what we have to do sometimes.

Here's the other thing about change: When you're in its midst, it's often hard to see what's in *front* of you, and even harder to see what's waiting for you down the road. When I divorced my first husband, for example, I would never have predicted in a million years that we would arrive at the point where we are today. My ex is a kind and loving father, always has been. My former and my current husband have even vacationed with my kids and me, together as a family.

During those dark days, when I was in the midst of my divorce (or the dark moments leading up to the divorce), I never would have predicted that I'd meet another man, a new mate, a best friend, who could make me so happy and lend so much meaning and substance to my life. But I did. My second husband, Greg, is the light of my life. He's a great father. He has a brilliant mind, not just in how he approaches business but in how he approaches life and living. He is patient and kind. He's even handy around the house! He has a great sense of humor, and he loves his family fiercely. As I was walking away from my first marriage, little did I know that I'd begun a journey that would guide me straight to him. That's how evolution works: it is constantly unfolding around us . . . even when we can't feel it.

Today, my children enjoy the rich benefits of a healthy co-parenting relationship, and are witness to a wonderful, real-life lesson they can see with their own eyes and feel with their own hearts: that out of something sad can come something that's very, very good. They *see* this now, with their own eyes, through their own little lenses. There's a leadership lesson in this, too: If you see that change is necessary—even if that change will be uncomfortable to make—you must believe in yourself (and your people) strongly enough to go ahead and make it. Furthermore, try not to operate in a vacuum. Before you make the change, enlist the feedback and ideas of those whose opinions and guidance you value. Make sure your decision is as well-informed and as thoroughly considered as possible. Then make the leap, take the plunge. *Cherish* the act of changing; do not shirk from it.

Figure out the ways you can become your very best self, and the ways your employees can become their very best selves, and if change is required to get you there, *then make it*. Also understand that where you stand now in your career, in your leadership, even in your day-to-day, moment-to-moment human existence, is not the same place you will be standing in, say, ten years, or even five. The organization you are leading now does not have to be your "forever place," nor should it be, necessarily. You will evolve. Your team will evolve. And with this evolution (both involuntary and of your own volition) will come growth that you never imagined.

Observing with this new lens is the best way to ensure that you will develop your employees in a way that they need and deserve to be developed. Always keep their growth in mind and always remember that growth is change, and change is evolution. Above all, remember that you have the right to be happy and fulfilled. You also have the responsibility, as a leader, to feed your employees a healthy diet of rich leadership that will make your organizational culture stronger, more forward-focused and, as a result, more solution-driven than problem-plagued.

All of this requires inner strength, resilience, and the confidence to respect the evolutionary process and to become an active agent of positive change. What basic leadership principles and characteristics will help guide you on this journey? There is one in particular that sets itself apart from all others. I see it as a shining beacon that will help illuminate your leadership journey, showing you the way ahead. It is what makes a good leader great and great leader extraordinary.

What is it?

Character.

5

Traits of the Greats: Character Matters

I INTENTIONALLY POSITIONED THIS CHAPTER smack-dab in the middle of the book because it is character that stands at the center of, well, of everything. Whether you're leading a business or living your life, character is what will bring meaning, value, and vision to the world around you. It is what guides us and what *centers* us. Therefore, this is precisely where this chapter belongs.

The beautiful thing about character is that it is made up of many notes. We don't all have to sing in an identical pitch; that would be impossible, and, frankly, not at all melodic. But in order to sing a leadership song that is rich, resonant, and harmonious, certain notes must be sung by us all.

Similarly, there are certain traits that make a great leader, i.e., specific notes that must be sung if we want to create a melody that is meaningful, visionary, and valuable. In this chapter, we'll explore what these "notes" sound like, what they look like in practice, what they feel like to sing. We will examine what it means to a culture or an organization to sustain these melodies and, conversely, what it looks like when those notes become discordant.

The character you bring to your leadership role is what helps form the culture of your company. Or, put more precisely, the character you bring to your leadership role is what helps *reflect* the culture of your company. How you lead helps set the standard. How you lead helps strike the tone. You are responsible for putting the notes on the page; it trickles down from you. The character of your employees is equally important, of course, but they take their cues from you, which means the lyrics of your leadership song must always be consistent, succinct, and resonant, and its lyrics must reflect and magnify the larger values of your culture and your organization.

Much like evolution, which we explored in the previous chapter, the act of character-building is ongoing and ever-changing. We must remain in a constant state of improvement—or, at least, awareness—as we develop and deepen our character. We must always take inventory by asking ourselves, "Am I being the very best leader I can be? Am I making the constant (and concerted) effort to reflect the values and vision of my organization in a way that my employees can clearly see, absorb, and emulate? Is the depth of my character demonstrated not just in my philosophical approach but in my daily actions as well? Am I singing this leadership song in a way that is true and authentic and reflects the organization that I am shepherding?

I realize that that's a long list of questions to ask yourself, but the good news is that, though there are plenty of questions, there is never one right answer for any of them. We are human beings, after all, unique in our personalities and preferences but united (hopefully) in our desire to bring the strongest *common* character traits to our leadership roles that we possibly can.

I've developed a shortlist of what I consider to be the most important of these character traits. These are traits that, when taken together, can help move a good leader towards being a great leader, or a not-so-great leader towards becoming a better leader. Again, the process is continuous. Like change itself, it is always in motion, always unfolding; therefore, we cannot avoid deepening our character and facilitating that growth in the people who surround us. It's an unstoppable process of self-discovery and growth.

Hitting the Right Notes

Throughout my career, the character traits that I've seen in other leaders have informed and guided me as I've honed my own leadership style and preferences. Yes, every human is unique and must sing his or her own leadership song. But certain common notes and melodies must ring loud and clear throughout the song. Otherwise, disharmony will happen—not just in your organization but in the larger world around you—because the consequences of our actions and our behaviors have a ripple effect that extends far beyond the workplace.

Take a careful look at this list of essential leadership characteristics: Are these notes ones that you are already singing, or might your songbook need to be expanded?

Note 1: Honesty (It's ALWAYS the Best Policy)

This one is a biggie. Instead of feeding you the answers (because there isn't just one right answer, as we already know), instead let's move through a list of questions about honesty. As you consider these questions, also ask yourself: Given that we all so deeply appreciate *receiving* honesty, why aren't we able to *give it* just as readily?

1. As a leader at work and a human at home, do you always speak the truth and behave honorably . . . even when no one's looking?

2. When you fall short (we all do occasionally), what tools and resources, both internal and external, do you have close at hand to guide you back on track and keep you in check? Can you trust yourself to self-correct?

3. How are you training your employees to be the most honorable humans they can possibly be? How has this been woven into the fabric of your organizational culture?

Note 2: Grit (Tap into It and Never Let It Go)

Entrepreneurs and young leaders, listen up, because this one is especially relevant to you, and I'm going to give it to you straight: "hard work" is . . . well, it's hard! Get in there and do it. No excuses. No pity parties. No turning back or easing off the accelerator just because you think it might be too difficult. Grit is determination, and determination is the will to succeed. You can't get to this place called success without having both.

When I was a young manager at Cisco (about twenty-five years old), and the company relocated me to Europe, I'll never forget the day I arrived. I felt disoriented, dispirited, and nowhere near as certain as I once was that this relocation was the right move for me. I was tired, lonely, hungry, and still a bit discombobulated from having to drive from the airport, after a twelve-hour flight, on the "wrong" side of the road . . . in a stick shift too, which was new to me! To top it all off, I locked myself out of my new flat. I remember the moment like it happened yesterday. I plopped down on the street curb, tears in my eyes, thinking, *Maybe I've made a mistake. Maybe this move just wasn't the right move for me. Maybe I'm not up to the task. I miss my home. I miss my fiancé. I'm not at all sure I even want to be here.* But in that same moment, because I must have already had the makings of a leader stirring within me, I forced myself to tap into that "gritty place" deep within me, the place that lived beyond my tears and that held within it my self-confidence, my resilience, and my determination to keep on keeping on, no matter what. Somehow, I stood up from that street curb, wiped my tears, and found a way to get into my new flat.

And somehow, in that moment, I launched my life as a leader.

I realize now, of course, that if I hadn't gotten to that gritty place, if I'd given up right there and flown back to the United States, I wouldn't be writing this book about leadership today. My trajectory would have been completely different. But because I didn't hightail it back home, I sit here now, writing about the importance of getting to that gritty place where tenacity and courage live, and finding a will and a way to put in the hard work all the time. No matter what.

The lesson here: Get to that gritty place whenever you need to. Know that it exists inside of you, always. If you lose it, find it again. Simple? Yes. Easy? Not always. But you must do it nonetheless.

Note 3: Humility (Resist the Urge to Always Be Right)

Constantly remind yourself that there is no such thing as perfection and, if there were, you certainly would not be it. As you are leading and living, remember that it's not about always being right; it's about always *doing* right.

As leaders, let's make sure we send the signal to our employees that we are keenly aware of our own flaws and foibles. When we bristle at criticisms being lodged against us, or when we find just a little *too* much pleasure in proving someone wrong, we shortchange ourselves, we shortchange the humans we are leading, and we ultimately shortchange the companies we work for.

If you haven't yet discovered how truly wonderful it feels to freely and openly admit to an employee, "You were right, and I was wrong. Thank you for teaching me," then it's time you find out. Furthermore, that truly wonderful feeling will heighten exponentially if you make this healthy admission of error in front of a group!

Note 4: Receptiveness

Closely linked to humility is openness. Here's what I call a "leadership myth": The most desirable workplace environment is one where everyone stands in agreement, no one causes dissension or dustups, and consensus reigns. In fact, this is not just a myth . . . *it's a mistake.*

Try, therefore, to resist the urge to surround yourself only with people who agree with you, i.e., employees who echo what they know you want to hear and are more interested in seeking your approval than expressing their own unique voices and concerns.

As is the case with virtually every aspect of leadership, though, there is an additional layer to explore, a deeper depth to dive into, an extra step to take to get us to greatness. We must do more than just resist surrounding ourselves with people who agree with our decisions. That's not enough by itself. Rather, we must learn to *actively seek* dissenting opinions and express an open desire to hear from those who have different ideas. This is what mature, responsible leadership looks like. A leader who is comfortable enough, confident enough, and intelligent enough to seek opinions different from their own is a leader who has learned how to move beyond their own interests, push past their own ego, and stand in a more expansive place.

We need to be careful with this one, though, because it is often our subconscious bias that tricks us into placing more value on the employee who is always agreeable and less value on the employee who brings in new ideas, who occasionally (and respectfully) rejects the status quo, and who will be brave enough to say, "Let's consider going up," when everyone else in the room is saying, "Let's go down."

Again, *mindset* comes into play. If we have already trained our brains to cultivate an environment where consensus is the goal, rather than a natural byproduct of thoughtful discussion, evaluation, and deliberation, then we have already lost the game. This mental rewiring of our "leadership brains" must be both conscious and continuous.

Retrain your brain so that it does not react negatively to pushback or feedback that is different from your viewpoint; learn not to take varying or opposing opinions as a personal affront or insult. This requires a deeper dive into your own subconscious. Why? Because so many of us have already conditioned ourselves into thinking—no, *believing*—that those who oppose or disagree with us are against us, when this is usually not the case at all.

Learn to get out of your own way and step away from your ego, your insecurities, and your need for approval. Asking the right questions might help you reframe this dynamic. Next time you sit down at the leadership table and you're trying to work through a new problem, a new project, or a new policy, consider asking these kinds of questions:

- What are we missing here? Where are the blind spots that we might have overlooked?
- Is there another direction, a different option, a fresh approach, that we haven't yet put onto the table? Who can offer us a different approach?
- Who amongst us would like to share a past encounter or life experience similar to what we're discussing that did not end positively? What did you learn then that might enlighten us now?
- What is your instinct telling you?

Note 5: Neutrality

This one is simple. Don't get caught up in the gossip game, the blame game, or the backbiting game. It's not just meanspirited, it is also totally unbecoming a leader, and I can guarantee the backbiting will eventually come back to bite *you*, too. That's not just a warning; it's an iron-clad promise. Like a boomerang, if you throw it out there, it is certain to come back.

The only way to succeed in this realm is to rise above petty politics and stay out of the fray, but there's another important component: rising above it is both noble and necessary, yes, but this is not sufficient by itself. As a leader, you must do more than rise. You must rise *and conquer* by canceling the culture that encourages such negativity in the first place. This means you must establish and enforce an environment of zero-tolerance for such nonsense.

If you see it or hear it happening, *call it out*. Take a stand. Discipline and/or remove employees who elect to play the game. Such behavior is detrimental and demoralizing. It creates ugly, discordant notes, which is not the kind of leadership song you want to be singing.

Remember that you are the person people look to for guidance and affirmation; you are the conductor of your symphony. You must set the stage, create the tone, and sustain the harmony. It will be the lyrics of your leadership song that ultimately reflect the values and vision of your company culture.

Note 6: Boldness

There's no avoiding this one. Uncomfortable situations will arise in the workplace that will invariably require your attention, your discernment, and your direct involvement. It's always best to address these issues head-on, up front, not only for the good (and the growth) of your employees but also as a way to explore and expand the depths of your leadership skills.

I think back to one of the first challenges I ever encountered as a young leader. I hadn't even officially started the job yet but had already been warned by my predecessor that a problematic employee in the group would need to be terminated immediately upon my arrival. Even when I think back on it, I can feel my hackles rising. Why would my predecessor put off handling a problem that obviously needed to be dealt with sooner rather than later? Why not address it and resolve it immediately, rather than letting it fester and deepen? Why wait for a new manager to handle an old issue that should already have been explored and/or addressed? I asked myself what I was getting myself into.

You can probably tell by now, as we journey deeper into the chapters of this book, that I am a no-nonsense person (and leader). I shoot straight, communicate succinctly, listen carefully, treat others with respect, dignity, and honor . . . and expect the same in return. When issues arise, I like to nip them in the bud quickly with both precision and compassion before they blossom into bigger, thornier problems. I give a lot and I expect a lot in return. This is how I am built.

One of my first meetings on the job was a big one. My entire staff—still new to me, obviously—was in attendance, along with several other division managers and, in fact, the CEO himself. Also in attendance was the woman I'd been "warned" about. I should also say here that, as a young manager and a new member of the team, I was prepared to give this employee the benefit of the doubt. I would not judge or act until I saw something from her that required my judgment or action. Put simply, I was not going to let the negative feedback I'd already received about her unduly influence or color my perception of her, not before we'd even had a chance to interact. I always want to be fair.

Unfortunately, during the meeting, something happened: *she fell asleep.* This was not a "let-me-close-my-eyes-for-a-moment-so-I-can-listen-more-intently" situation. She was asleep. No two ways about it. Immediately after the meeting, I took her aside and addressed her directly but respectfully. I told her that if she wanted to continue to grow in her job, which I hoped she did, and if she was planning to be successful in her professional pursuits, and I certainly hoped she was, then falling asleep in any meeting (especially a meeting with the CEO in attendance) was simply not an option.

I also told her that if it happened again, or if it became clear that she was unable or unwilling to perform the duties and requirements of her job, she would be terminated. I urged her to think about and explore, in her own mind, what other issues might be at play; perhaps there was something she was missing in this equation, a wrinkle in this problem, of which she simply was not yet aware.

As it turned out, she went to the doctor shortly thereafter and made an important discovery: she was severely diabetic. The diabetes was what was causing her extreme fatigue. She came to me after her doctor's appointment filled with emotion, and if I were asked to identify which emotion she displayed most prominently, the response would be easy: *gratitude*. She thanked me for being straightforward but respectful. She thanked me for handling an uncomfortable situation with dignity, compassion, and grace. She thanked me for "waking her up"—in more ways than one. She also thanked me for saving her life. Today, we are still in touch with each other. She still calls me for career advice and guidance; we even share information and updates on our respective families. I am glad we've remained in touch.

The leadership lesson here is this: We must learn to push through uncomfortable situations until we get through to the other side of that discomfort to a place of resolution and mutual understanding. Procrastination is not an option. Neither is subpar or unacceptable performance.

As always, there's another, deeper layer nestled within this leadership lesson, too: Your employees need, want, and deserve your feedback on a regular basis. If this employee had received feedback from her previous manager, even negative feedback, at least she would have been able to respond to it. To act on it. To attempt to improve, address, or resolve it. If feedback of any kind had been offered earlier, the situation might have been minimized. This leads us gracefully towards yet another topic that is not always readily discussed but is certainly worthy of discussion and worthy of *action*: feedback.

Note 7: Constructiveness

For a variety of reasons, managers and leaders are often reticent to give their employees meaningful and continuous feedback. There is a general hesitancy, I've noticed, to go beyond (or deeper than) the annual and/or quarterly reviews. Push yourself to do better.

As it turns out, the employee who fell asleep in the meeting happened to be in a protected class—*three* protected classes, actually. She was Black, over forty, and female. Understand that the manager who doesn't provide open, honest feedback to each and every employee, regardless of their protected class or status, is doing that employee and the organization itself a grave disservice.

Understand this, too. When you hesitate to give negative feedback to an employee simply because of their protected status, when your failure to be completely honest stems from fear of possible legal repercussions, you're not really protecting your organization at all. You're hurting it. Everyone should be treated with equal respect, dignity, and honor, but if malfeasance, mediocrity, or continued missteps occur, face them head-on. When you don't, everyone loses.

We need to look at feedback not as a quarterly duty or an annual, paperwork-driven obligation, but as an ongoing investment in our people; it should, therefore, become a constant part of our organizational culture. Without it, how else will your team be led and guided? How else will they know when to adjust and/or recalibrate?

Also, feedback works both ways. When your employees don't feel comfortable or safe providing feedback about how you are conducting yourself as a leader, how will *you* know when you've fallen short or slipped up or even done something wonderful? (Feedback should not always be negative.) When we invest in a culture that encourages and facilitates feedback, we invest in our people, which is precisely what every organization is made up of: people. Decide to make the investment.

I'm in three protected categories myself: female, disabled, and over forty. Yet I still fully expect, want, and need to be able to receive open, honest, and continuous feedback, not just from the people I work for but the people I work with. This is the definition of a healthy organizational culture.

What kind of culture do you want to create?

Note 8: Bravery

It is often the worst experiences that produce the most valuable and enduring lessons. I strongly believe that we can learn just as much from a bad leader as we can from a good one—perhaps even more. Knowing what *not* to do often informs and guides our thinking as we evaluate what *to* do moving forward. This is true in leadership as well as and in life.

I'm going *way* back to my first real relationship here. I was a teenager, around fifteen years old. Like many young teenagers, I was hungry for attention but unsure of myself. I often felt vulnerable and afraid. I still didn't fully understand what a loving, nurturing relationship looked or felt like, primarily because I hadn't really seen any in my own household.

Unfortunately, the first person with whom I became romantically involved wasn't a great guy. In fact, he was less than great; he was awful. He quickly became controlling, demanding, jealous, and domineering. Even when the relationship became abusive, I stayed in it. I realize now, though, I don't regret that I stayed so long. I used to feel embarrassed and disappointed in myself for suffering through the pain and indignity for as long as I did, but I no longer feel that way. I have evolved my thinking. Today, I realize that I learned vital, enduring life lessons from that relationship; lessons I was able to bring with me to my leadership experience.

Yes, it took me a while to extricate myself, and it took an extraordinary amount of courage (especially at that young age), but I eventually did walk away from that toxic relationship and did not look back. When I did walk away, I walked away without fearing the repercussions because I knew that staying would be worse than leaving, and leaving was what needed to happen. I pushed myself through an incredibly uncomfortable situation and ended up on its other side.

That profoundly negative experience taught me profoundly positive lessons. I learned much about what kindness is by seeing what kindness is *not*. I know precisely what kindness looks like today; I know its depth and its breadth, and I know it intimately.

That I was guided towards a husband today who is so immensely kind, so gentle and loving, and so much of everything that I need and want out of life is all the more precious to me because I have known the flip side of kindness, too. Today, I know kindness in all its fullness.

Isn't this what leadership is all about? What *character* is all about? Being mature enough, thoughtful enough, and responsible enough to be able to draw from the depths of our earlier experiences, even the bad experiences, in a way that lets us appreciate their fullness? I have learned from the not-so-great managers I've had throughout my career as much as I've learned from the great ones. What kind of leader do you want to be? What will you do with the tools and the traits we've just explored in this chapter? Which of these character traits do you need to work on, explore, embrace?

*

Our leadership journey is never-ending. We are constantly growing, deepening, expanding, improving, and evolving. The road just keeps on unfolding and stretching out before us. I see it as a good thing: this is a promise of continued growth.

We've peeled back the layers of leadership where character lives. What will you do with them now?

6

Democratizing Opportunity

THE TOPIC OF CREATING EQUITABLE opportunity and the subject of remote work (which we'll examine in the next chapter) go hand in hand. They complement and facilitate each other, but in this chapter, we're going to pull apart their common threads in order to get an aerial view, then we'll drill down from there.

Let's first look at the vital importance of creating equitable opportunity in our workplaces and our communities as a leadership principle. I strongly believe that an examination of the principle itself should come first, followed by a deeper dive, in the next chapter, into the tools and practices we can use to actually *get to* this place of expanded opportunity. (Spoiler alert: What will get us to a place of expanded opportunity, as you've probably already guessed, *is* remote work—that's why the sequence of these two chapters is so important.)

Let's start with good news.

The act of redistributing opportunity is well within our reach. We just need to teach ourselves how to *reach* for it. As leaders, we must remind ourselves that we have the ability and the wherewithal to set this process of redistributing opportunity into motion. It is doable . . . but to do it means we've got to decide to, well, get it done.

This will take action, a purposeful shift in mindset, followed by a forward momentum that will facilitate positive change. Rather than just talking about these concepts in meetings and writing about them in books (I'm referring to myself here, obviously), we have the power, through our policies, our actions, and a newly expanded leadership vision, to move these ideas out into the real world! This part is worth repeating: We can get this work done; we just need to decide that it's worth doing . . . then do it.

Why *wouldn't* we want to expand opportunity in a way that creates a positive impact, not just in the workplace but also in our communities, our families, our towns, and the larger world around us? We need to look at this as far more than a pleasant option, as far more than a frilly, feel-good principle. In a very real way, the principle (and practice) of distributing opportunity more equitably is our responsibility and our obligation. This is real-world stuff.

So, although this and the next chapter belong to each other thematically, let's begin with a look at the principle first, and understand that if we are to embrace this principle, it might require us to peel back the layers more methodically.

A Powerful New Paradigm

I've seen what it looks like to expand opportunity in the work-place; I've had a bird's eye view. Every single experience I've had in the world of remote work (and there have been many of them, most long before the arrival of the pandemic) has led me to the rock-solid conclusion that we can and should be doing more to reopen the clogged lanes of opportunity that exist in our workplaces and in the world itself.

Here's the macro view: As leaders, we are faced with the unique opportunity, perhaps today more than any other time in history, *to democratize opportunity*. To fully embrace this concept, we will need to undergo a shift in our leadership philosophy and overall approach. There are ways we can go about the task (and meet the obligation) to democratize opportunity, but as I mentioned, it requires a broader perspective.

A closer examination of this principle will open our eyes to a critical piece of information that many of us have been missing. Namely, that it is *opportunity* that needs to be distributed more evenly, *not wealth*. Too often we get these twisted up. We must understand that there is plenty of talent throughout this wide, wide world of ours, but although ability and talent are distrib-uted evenly across the planet, opportunity is not.

Technology and software companies in particular are uniquely positioned to redistribute opportunity in groundbreaking and strikingly innovative ways that can shift the world on its axis and change the way we work, live, and exist. We stand, today, at the precipice of opportunity to create further opportunity. As leaders, we are in the unique position of tapping into this potential in a way that can have a far-reaching and extraor-dinary impact. We can be the pebble in a pond that creates waves and ripples that will be felt not just in the workplace but in the lives and homes and hearts of our employees, in our own communities and across the globe. As leaders, this is our responsibility. Let's step up.

The way we step up to this challenge is by focusing on people and communities first, rather than filling up a building with employees or seeing your company name and/or logo emblazoned on the top of a building. This is when you begin to have a positive impact on the world around you. (Plus, it will ultimately bring bottom-line benefits to your company.)

As a businessowner, a senior executive, and an entrepreneur myself, I am certainly not saying that profit is unimportant; such a statement would be foolish, short-sighted, and not at all realistic. What I *am* saying, though, is that by putting our people first, we are setting ourselves up more efficiently and effectively to create a cycle of productivity, satisfaction, engagement, human connection, and general sense of well-being that brings benefit to everyone involved. People run our companies; profits do not. It's important to remind ourselves on a regular basis that profit and revenue should never exist in a vacuum. They should never be the solitary goal, to the exclusion of all else. When we lead with a profit-first, rather than a people-first mindset, we are not leading with grace. We are leading with greed.

The notion that we, as leaders, can make a substantial and enduring difference in the world around us, in addition to making a difference in the companies we lead, is higher-order thinking. The realization that we can have an extraordinarily positive impact not just on how we work and live today but also on how we'll work and live *tomorrow* is revelatory in itself . . . yet many leaders haven't yet taken the time to expand their vision in a way that will allow them to embrace the potential and power that we hold.

It's time to change all that.

It's time to open our eyes to our own potential. It is this potential, combined with purposeful action, of course, that will change the landscape of the workplace and the world as we know it.

This is a leadership principle, then, of the highest order. And it will require a shift in our mindset.

The Beauty of Balance

Part of adopting this "higher order" mindset involves ridding ourselves of some outdated notions that are no longer relevant in today's fast-evolving world and workplace.

We often hear people talk about the importance of establishing and maintaining a more comfortable "work-life balance" as the way to put us on the path towards success, fulfillment, and, ultimately, happiness. My reaction? Let's be a little more expansive and sophisticated in our thinking. When we focus on a work-life balance, we're missing the point. It's not about balancing work and life as much as it is *integrating* the two. It's time to accept that work is a part of our lives. When we go to work every day, for instance, we do not stop living the rest of our lives. This is the reality: work is part of life.

Being able to work in newer, more adaptive environments (e.g., remote work), we allow people to live their best lives, their most fully integrated lives, which leads to healthier relationships, stronger communities, greater employee engagement, and greater productivity. Why not let people live where they want to live instead of living where they have to work?

During my days as an executive at GitLab, for example, it was amazing for me to be able to coach my daughter's soccer team. GitLab, as you'll remember from earlier chapters, is a completely remote-work company that afforded me extraordinary opportunities I never could have conceived or imagined had I remained in the strict confines of a brick-and-mortar work environment. Working remotely meant that I no longer had to struggle with the hour-and-a-half commute each way, meaning that I no longer wasted so many unproductive hours stuck in bumper-to-bumper traffic.

Instead, after putting in a full day of work from home (working with extraordinary talent across the globe, I should add, because this is what working remotely makes possible), I still had the time, the energy, and the *desire* to get to the soccer field and be present not just for my daughter but also an entire team of young women who were depending on me to be there. I was fully present for them ... and I was fully present for myself as well. I wasn't all that *great* a soccer coach, by any means, but that wasn't really the issue at all. What mattered was that, because I was now an executive in a company that had a bold, innovative, and workable vision that embraced the concept of remote work, I had been afforded bold, innovative, workable *options* that improved the quality of my life on virtually every level.

When employees can interact, thrive, and contribute to the communities where they live (and work), opportunity can be distributed more evenly. Why should we continue to drain communities of their most precious resources—their people—by requiring them to leave those communities in order to make a living? Leaving communities intact, allowing human connections and meaningful relationships to remain strong, while still fostering a healthy remote work environment provides the opportunity to live meaningful, fully integrated lives, on every conceivable level.

Being able to work remotely was transformative, especially at a time in my life when I was facing serious health challenges, still trying to find my way in the world with a new job that was unlike any job I'd held before, and still finding my footing as a single mom. We'll explore the layers and levels of remote work in the upcoming chapter, but since my own experiences at GitLab had such a profound effect on how I see leadership today, I thought it was both important and instructive to unpack the benefits of redistributing opportunity.

1. Because the executives at GitLab were so fully and boldly committed to their vision, I could be there for them a hundred percent. Because I was allowed to be both a fully present employee and a fully present parent, the company reaped the benefits of hiring an executive (me) who was highly engaged, highly productive, and just plain *happy*.

2. The local community benefitted because I worked where I lived and was, therefore, funneling more of my tax dollars directly back into my community by supporting and frequenting local businesses.

3. My daughter benefited, of course, from having a mom who could also serve as the team soccer coach. I could also be there for my daughter, on the soccer field, with her teammates, coaching them face-to-face, without struggling with feelings of guilt about having to leave the office early.

4. Our household benefited, even, because that feeling of human connection and cohesion was strengthened far more than it would have been if I'd been away from home for most of the day (and the evening, given the interminable commute).

What I'm drawing here is an illustration of how this leadership principle and, indeed, the very act of redistributing opportunity can bring benefits to everyone involved. Everybody wins. Perhaps I won the most because the opportunity given to me helped me become the very best version of myself.

This is what I mean when I talk about how we, as leaders, can create innovative new opportunities for our people so that they are able to lead the very best lives they can possibly lead. In my case, I was fortunate to be actively recruited by a cutting-edge, groundbreaking company, the likes of which I'd never seen, whose corporate culture fully embraced and embodied the notion that work and life are not to be balanced but integrated, and they did so with skill, dexterity, intention, and bold new vision. The "pebble," then, that was dropped by the visionary GitLab execs created ripple effects that led to greater employee satisfaction, more meaningful family and community interactions, higher employee engagement, and a deeper sense of human connection, contentment, and well-being that was (and is) good for everyone involved.

Test the Water

Before we do a deeper dive into the realities (and, in my mind, still-untapped potential) of remote work, I want to return to a concept I introduced at the outset of this chapter, because understanding and embracing this concept is absolutely essential.

We already know that the world around us, particularly since the arrival of COVID-19, has been forever changed. Companies learned to become more innovative because they were *forced* to if they wanted to survive. Now that we seem to have suffered through the worst of the pandemic, now that it has loosened its cruel death grip in a way that allows us to reflect and regroup, we realize—or *should* realize—that the demand for innovation is not simply going to disappear. It will remain. Innovation is here to stay.

For this reason alone, then, we know that we will not be running out of opportunity anytime soon. If innovation is here to stay (which it is), so is opportunity. Look at today's workforce: we can't seem to find enough workers! This tells us, then, that opportunity is not a scarce resource. It is abundant. This should also tell us that making opportunity more equally accessible will be the key to our success moving forward, both on a global and a human scale.

As leaders, we need to envision a working world where we are able to keep our employees connected to the other parts of their lives that are meaningful and important: connected to their families, their communities, and to the people, places, and things that are enduring and anchoring. The person with a happy life is also the employee with higher productivity and greater engagement. The two things go hand in hand. There is a way for us to facilitate this process. There are tools and techniques we can deploy that will not only ensure that we remain innovative but also ensure that our employees remain content and connected to the things that matter most to them at the same time. It should not be an either-or proposition. *It can be both.*

We've examined the importance of expanding opportunity, primarily as a leadership principle. Now it's time to move from principle to practice, and the way we do that is by unpacking the reality of remote work: it is the key to our future.

We already know, from having traveled through the darkness of the pandemic and from being forced to adopt new working patterns, that remote work is here to stay, in some form. We already figured out ways to make remote working *work* because we had to; there was no other option. Today, we stand at the precipice and have a choice to make. We have the tools; we just have to learn to use them correctly. Indeed, remote work *can* work if our approach is thoughtful, smart, and strategic. And don't worry, you won't have to move at lightning speed; you can move in small, comfortable increments. Start with baby steps and work your way up to a remote work model that is most comfortable for you and your company. Perhaps you can start by dipping your toe in. It needn't be a full swan dive.

The more you know about remote work—how to do it right, the drawbacks of doing it wrong—the more meaningful your journey will become. The most important thing is to see what you can learn. We already know, from having made it through the storm of the pandemic, that we can survive. Now, armed with knowledge, experience, and foresight, we must do more than merely survive. We must *thrive*.

The world is waiting, so let's dip that toe right in. As we're about to learn in this next chapter, the water is just fine.

7

Remote Work Works

I'LL READILY ADMIT THAT BEFORE I fully experienced the world of remote work for myself, the *idea* of remote work was just that: remote. The concept was abstract, insubstantial, relevant only for jobs that didn't require collaboration with other people.

I've already recounted in earlier chapters how the possibility of working in a digital environment was not something I'd ever envisioned for myself. In fact, I was as surprised as anyone when the opportunity to step into the world of remote work was presented. Not until the executives at GitLab set their sights on me, then actively recruited me, then warmly welcomed me into their groundbreaking, cutting-edge, completely remote organizational culture did I see firsthand the extraordinary benefits that a world like this could bring. It was, in a single word, *awesome*.

My transition from Netflix to GitLab was smooth, but it was not without strong emotion. Now that I look back on it, I realize that the hodge-podge of emotions I experienced—fear, anxiety, confusion, gratitude, excitement—were precisely the emotions I was *supposed* to experience. Each emotion had a reason for being, and I respect each and every one of them. It's worth noting here that, as leaders, we sometimes tend to overlook the value and validity of our emotions. We've trained our brains to focus instead on the solidity of cold, hard facts and bottom-line, cut-and-dried conclusions. These are certainly important, of course, but here are my words of wisdom, shared from the depth of my own experience: *Learn to honor and respect your emotions, too.* We are humans first, leaders second. Our instincts and emotions can inform us and guide us every bit as effectively (in some cases, more effectively) than the endless flurry of spread sheets, pie charts, and data analyses that are so often put before us. As leaders, we must learn to rely on both facts *and* emotions. The beauty is in the balance.

When making major decisions, either in our personal lives or in our lives of leadership, listening to and honoring our emotions is essential; it should not be perceived as a sign of weakness or indecision. In fact, being able to balance the facts in our brain and the emotions in our heart is extremely helpful when we must make life-changing decisions. This balance often gives us the momentum we need to move forward, and it often pushes us towards taking an action that's not always easy to take.

That's how we should look at our deeper dive into the world of remote work: it will require a leap of faith. It will require a healthy trust in ourselves as capable, courageous, competitive leaders who want only the best for our companies and our employees. It is a decision based on fact and empirical knowledge, but it is also an emotional decision. The sooner we recognize and establish this balance, the better off we'll be.

Let this be of comfort to you, too. We've all been forced to adopt some sort of remote model in our workplaces during the storm of the global pandemic. We've all been exposed to the phenomenon of remote work. We know what it feels like. Why not continue moving forward? Why not push forward into more progressive work patterns and offer your employees greater freedom and greater opportunity? Ask yourself what kind of leader you want to be: do you want to be a leader who embraces positive change rather than stands still in its midst? Or so you want to be one who reverts back to the old-school ways of working, even when a better alternative has been presented?

I was certainly reluctant initially. But I ultimately allowed myself to honor each of the emotions that swirled around me as I walked towards this Strange New World at GitLab. Rather than getting bogged down or paralyzed by these emotions, I *leaned into them*, and this is what helped give me the momentum I needed to embrace my new position at GitLab with confidence, courage, and grace. This is also what allowed me to deal with the long, sad farewells as I left my colleagues at Netflix. This is what helped make my transition, not only away from Netflix but into the digital world, less tumultuous. I was able to make the transition swiftly, too, and "rip off the Band-Aid," as the saying goes. It still hurt like hell because I loved my job at Netflix more than I'd ever loved any job, but I had no choice but to leave. The long commute and the required travel presented potential challenges that were virtually insurmountable with my health issues. Plus, traveling to New York City for treatment and undergoing chemotherapy would have simply been too much on top of everything else. It wasn't worth the risk to me, my family, and Netflix as a company.

I suppose it's accurate to say that during that scary, uncertain time in my life, I was struggling with sickness on a couple of different levels. I was struggling with the physical sickness of disease, of course, but I was struggling with an emotional sickness as well; it broke my heart to have walk away from the most exciting job I'd ever had in my professional career, working with some of the most brilliant minds in the industry and, indeed, the world. This is what happens in both life and in leadership, though, and what I'm going to say next is far, far more than a mere cliché: when one door closes, another door (at *least* one) always opens. The tricky part is that we have no idea of what's waiting for us on the other side of that door until we actually walk through it. How would I have ever known, before I walked through the "virtual doors" of GitLab, that my life would be changed, my relationships deepened, my connections to other humans strengthened in ways I could never have imagined? I didn't . . . until I got there.

So, what started out as a transition made out of necessity, what began as tentative step into a new world I knew absolutely nothing about, has turned into my super-passion.

Today, my super-passion is remote work.

It's Here to Stay

Working at GitLab taught me that it is possible to build strong, enduring employee connections digitally. The experience also taught me that amazing talent has no borders. Granted, I found the extraordinary Narnia-like world of remote work more by accident than intention, but the lessons I learned once I walked through the wardrobe remain rich and enduring. That all of this happened well before COVID-19 slammed headlong into our world actually creates some interesting parallels that I hope will be highly instructive.

Of this much we are certain: Our experience with remote work during the pandemic was nowhere near as engaging and rewarding as our experience with remote work during better times. Why? Because we were forcefully shoved towards the remote work model during the pandemic. We didn't have a *choice* . . . not if we wanted to survive. The good news is that now we've arrived at this new place, now that we've seen some of the extraordinary benefits of this new work model (which will increase exponentially as we become more thoughtful in our approach and practice), we realize that there is really no turning back. Remote work is here to stay. So, why *wouldn't* we do all that we can to learn more about it? To strengthen and refine whatever models we might have "resorted to" initially in a way that will help us grow, expand, and become better leaders today and tomorrow?

We have emerged from the darkness of the pandemic, thank goodness, but now our task is to take what we learned as a result of having pushed through that darkness and refine it in a way that brings value to the companies and humans that we lead.

Liberation

When I think about the ways remote work has opened up the world for us, when I think about how its arrival has made things that were once impossible *possible*, I think of the extraordinary talent I've been able to recruit from across the globe—talent that would otherwise have been impossible to attract because the physical barriers were not only daunting but deal-breaking.

I also think of one of my employees at GitLab, who was as bright, as sharp, and as spirited as they come. As much as she had to offer, as brilliant a mind as she had, Brittany would simply not have been able to bring her talent to a traditional, brick-and-mortar office setting. Why? Because she was also a military wife, which meant that every time her husband was transferred to a new military base, she had to move with him. (I should add here that she didn't just *have* to move, she *wanted* to move, to keep her family intact! It was a purposeful and necessary choice on her part.) Of course, the constant relocations made it difficult—if not *impossible*—for her to stay at one company long enough to set down roots, establish a consistent employee history, and, perhaps most importantly, secure a long-term path towards the professional growth and advancement she certainly deserved.

But what was impossible yesterday has become possible today. I was able to recruit Brittany into the remote working world of GitLab, and in that space, she flourished tremendously. It didn't *matter* if her husband was transferred to a new location, because she was able to "show up" at work no matter where she was in the world! What it meant was that she wasn't forced to make a choice between building a career and being fully present for (and with) her husband and two young children as they moved and grew and transitioned.

GitLab's forward-thinking remote work environment allowed her to have it all, in the most literal sense. And not only did she survive in that completely remote workspace, she thrived beautifully. She was hired originally as an entry-level employee but rose at a sure and steady rate to become a director of the company.

That's what remote work can offer: flexibility, adaptability, growth, and advancement, regardless of location. It opens up our world.

Brittany was able to thrive fully, live completely, grow exponentially, and become the very best version of herself she could possibly become because GitLab was committed to a culture that facilitates and invites that kind of growth. Its leaders were (and are) committed to nourishing this culture, not just because it brings benefit and growth to their employees but because it brings benefit and growth to the company itself.

I also want to point out here that Brittany is someone I've stayed in contact with since leaving GitLab. Even today, I still speak with her fairly frequently. In fact, I'm in much closer contact with my former colleagues at GitLab than I am with those from any of my earlier jobs, which is proof positive that a digital work environment often creates and fosters strong, enduring relationships—quite the outcome, given the fact we never saw each other face-to-face in the workplace! There were no daily "water cooler conversations" or shared moments in the conference room, sitting side by side, sharing the same physical space. To be honest, the notion that your employees *must all* assemble at the same gleaming conference table or squeeze themselves into the same room for that all-hands morning meeting is becoming embarrassingly old-school. It's outdated. Not only outdated but also counterproductive.

This alternative way to live that is far more efficient, far less expensive, and far more hospitable for employees, families, and communities. However, it requires us, as leaders, to adopt (or at least expand) a new leadership model that forces us to think and behave more ambitiously. The leadership lesson here, of course, is that if you expand your boundaries, if you open not just your mind but also your workplace in a way that embraces this new way of interacting, communicating, and *being*, then you create opportunities for growth that you never could have imagined. You will be able to hire the best people wherever they happen to live in the world, be it a tiny little town in Dubuque, an economically challenged neighborhood in Detroit, or a bustling community in Delhi. I have personally hired amazing employees throughout the world, including Nigeria and Russia, whom I simply wouldn't have been able to recruit in a traditional brick-and-mortar environment.

I should also point out that this ability to hire your employees from wherever they are in the world will enhance the diversity within your organization, as well and provide extraordinary opportunity for people who wouldn't normally have had such opportunities. Again, everyone benefits.

Will such expansion and redefinition of the workplace bring challenges and complications? Of course it will, just because it is new. But until we *do it*, until we educate and inform ourselves more intelligently about the process itself, and until we wade a little deeper in this new water, until we take that leap of faith (the balance between the emotions in our heart and the empirical facts before us), we will not be able to fully and completely reap the benefits in any meaningful or enduring way.

Home Court Advantage

The sooner you can expand your leadership vision so that it looks beyond the four walls of your office and the physical footprint of your office building, the better your employees will be, your company will be, and the world around you will be. I'm not advocating a sudden and total transformation to remote work—that wouldn't be wise for many reasons—but it's time to begin incorporating major elements of this new model into your company culture on a permanent, sustainable basis. Look at it as a much-needed generational change.

Before the pandemic changed the working world as we know it, we'd only known our employees, our cohorts, our colleagues, our bosses, and even our interns on a segmented, superficial level. We only got to see the slice of their lives that they brought with them to the office. Nothing more, nothing less. With remote work, we are given a much richer, much more resonant portrait of the humans with whom we work. Today, when we sit down to meet with our teams in a digital environment, we are given an intimate glimpse into their lives and the comfort of their own homes. We get to take a peek at what color schemes they like; we sometimes even get to meet their children and their pets! Leaders: Doesn't this more multi-dimensional glimpse add more depth and texture to our understanding and appreciation of the humans who make up our companies? I'll help you with the answer. The answer is "yes."

A word of warning, though. Working from home is not the ideal workspace for every single person. For this reason, it will be important to help these employees develop other alternatives. Community-based coworking spaces, like local libraries might be considered. Private companies also provide a workspace for those who prefer not to work from their own homes. The good news is that options abound.

As a leader in the field of remote work, particularly the human-resource aspects of remote work, what I have also noticed is that many leaders and companies tend to *over-engineer* their approach to working at home. Don't be too hard on your employees as they continue to navigate the "newness" and the challenges of working from their living room instead of their office. Give them some space to adapt. Remember that they are working within the space where they *live*, which may be a huge adaptation for some. Try not to be critical of the occasional crying child, ringing doorbell, or barking dog. This is when we should open our minds and our hearts and view these glimpses into real lives not as interruptions but as ways we can get to know our employees and teammates better!

The long and short of it is this: be patient with the process. Seek help, externally and internally, from remote-work experts who can guide you in this process. Remember that you do not (and should not) take this journey alone. Rely on those who know to help lead you. Leaders can be led, too.

All that said, it should be noted that even in the world of remote work, social engagement is still important. I recommend, when it's physically possible, still meeting socially, just to have the occasional benefit of that face-to-face interaction. And when physical gatherings are impossible, I recommend having weekly or daily "social" calls. The point, here, is that we need to build social interactions into online interactions on a consistent basis, whilst taking care not to make these interactions feel too transactional. Again, there is a balance, and that balance will be more comfortably achieved over time.

As Chief People Officer at LoveToKnow, an online media company, for instance, we called these meetings "Coffee and Cab" and they worked beautifully. ("Cab" referred to those who preferred a glass of wine). Of course, this didn't advocate daytime drinking! It was called this because employees worked in different time zones, so it meant that at the same moment of day, some of us were waking up to our morning coffee and some of us were settling down to a nice glass of wine.

Other options for social interaction with your employees could involve setting up messaging apps and channels (such as Slack), encouraging employees who might share similar outside interests to set up online social groups, and encouraging employees to share parenting or other life challenges (or successes) in non-office settings. You can even play games on Zoom, for example, which is a wonderful way to kick back, get to know one another, and have fun together at the same time! Again, turn to those who have experience with this for input and guidance. Seek help from those who can provide it.

The point is this: What we are being given with remote work (and what we are giving our teammates and employees) is the opportunity to grow, develop, and lean into the joy of working where we live. It's bold. It's brave. We already know how to do it. Now the task before us is refining and expanding this base of knowledge . . . then *acting* on it, of course.

As leaders, we can learn so much more about our employees—and our employees can learn so much more about us—if we open our minds to the belief that remote work really *can* work, and if we open our hearts to the possibility that human relationships can actually be deepened in this digital environment in ways we never imagined. That we can do all of this while sitting in the comfort of our own home (or wherever your remote work base happens to be) is icing on the cake. Our homes are what help make us human, and our humanity is what helps makes our organizations living, breathing entities.

However, let's be sensitive to this fact, too, as we move forward: It is important to acknowledge that not all roles and not every industry can adopt the remote work model successfully. Some jobs require human-to-human contact, plain and simple. But when those of us who *can* work remotely *do* work remotely, it is far better for those who must still drive into the office, if only because their commute will be eased by fewer vehicles jamming our streets and interstates, to say nothing of the environmental benefits that come from having fewer cars on the road. This I would describe as *a cycle of positive impact that brings benefit to everyone.*

What remote work offers, then, is the opportunity for enduring human connections—a notion that, in and of itself, sounds a bit contradictory. What this means is that we have opportunity to learn more about ourselves and each other, both from the heart and from the home.

If that's not a home-court advantage, then I don't know what is.

When Remote Work Doesn't Work

The drawbacks and downfalls that come with remote work will only come for one reason: if you're not utilizing it correctly. I actually consider this *good* news, not just because it places priority on using your work model as efficiently and thoughtfully as you possibly can, but because it offers you a sense of ownership and accountability moving forward.

Put simply, the only reason remote work will fail in our organizations is if we are missing some angle, or creating some imbalance, or overlooking some nuance, that we should have seen but didn't. But do not be discouraged. There are ways to correct any problem, methods to address any challenge. It all starts with awareness, as I often like to say, and simply being aware of some of the potential pitfalls is the first principle of avoiding them.

Here are the challenges that are most common in the world of remote work. Chances are high that you've encountered some in your organization already, given that most of us have already become somewhat accustomed to this new way of working and living.

Coexisting Cultures

Remember that a remote work environment offers us the opportunity to unite continents and countries in a way that we've never been able to before. This is a wonderful opportunity to recruit and manage people from an almost limitless number of different cultures, which is a wonderful thing in itself but means we must we make a purposeful, constant effort to recognize and appreciate these different backgrounds in a way that honors the individual and respects their culture as much as possible. This will require on our part an expanded vision and a wider embrace—both good ideas yet we must remember to *act on* them.

Language barriers might be an issue, and even seemingly innocuous (but actually very important) uses of phrases and vernacular that are acceptable and/or unacceptable based on culture, preference, etc. It will require awareness, flexibility, respect, and dexterity.

Under this category, of course, also falls national holidays, religious holidays, which should be noted and honored as far as possible.

The most important message in all of this, of course, is *awareness*. As our work world expands to include more cultures on a global scale, so also should our overall awareness.

Organization Culture-Fit

In addition to respecting and honoring the cultures of our global employees, however, comes the equally important factor that every employee must ultimately respect, uphold, and adhere to the culture, the vision, and the values of the organization itself.

Just because we now have the expanded capacity to widen and enhance our cultural diversity doesn't mean we forget to honor the company culture. It is the company culture—i.e., what we believe as an entity and how we conduct our business—that is the heartbeat of the company itself. With respect to company culture, there should be no deviation.

Two types of cultural respect must be afforded here. Make sure you are able to make the distinction, and set clear rules for observing both.

Time Zone Logistics

A second potential challenge when it comes to bringing different cultures, countries, and global communities together is being aware of how many time zones need to be crossed during a typical workday. Try to be respectful of everyone's location and everyone's rhythm. This will increase the need to collaborate asynchronously. Keep in mind that you don't need to solve all of these logistical problems yourself. Turn to (and *talk* to) others, internally and externally, for guidance. See how others do it. Brainstorm, share information, and solicit the opinions of those who know.

Establishing Trust

Working, managing, and leading in a remote environment will definitely require a higher level of trust, but try not to get trust confused with *control*. Trust and control are two different things. If you feel like you need to install sophisticated spyware or digital software on your employee's computers to monitor how many hours or minutes they're spending on work-related activities, that's not an issue with trust; it's an issue of distrust. And it's also an issue of control.

No leader should ever have to try to control or force their employees to get their work done. The work should be getting done regardless of where they are. And if the work isn't getting done in way that is serving the company, this is more of a management issue than anything else.

You should know your people well enough—and know the tasks involved in their job well enough—to be able to assess whether the job is being performed satisfactorily. You don't have to be a better manager to manage a remote work environment, but if you're not a good manager to begin with, it's going to show.

Many companies have manager training on how to manage effectively in a remote environment. The resources exist, internally and externally. Be a responsible leader and avail yourselves of these resources. You're going to need help along this journey, so be the strong manager that you are and *ask for* that help.

Controlled Take Off

I've mentioned this before, but it's worth repeating: it is neither strategic nor wise to bite off more than you chew. Remember that you can start slowly in this world of remote work and increase your pace and your frequency from there.

You'll remember I mentioned in the chapter Never Give Up that I'm studying to become a licensed pilot. Any new pilot, or anyone in training to *become* a new pilot, knows they must take their first flights in the small "puddle-jumper" plane, rather than the large passenger jets. (Thankfully, FAA rules prevent new pilots from flying the larger planes.) This gradual upgrade, this slow ascension from small plane to mammoth flying machine, is purposeful and strategic. The same principles apply as you glide into the world of remote work. Take it easy. Take it slow. Don't start with the Boeing 777 before you master the Cessna 152.

Lots of managers will try a modified version of remote work with their team members for a period of time, just to see how people adjust to the new practice. This gradual approach is the most human (and humane!) way to fly into the friendly skies of remote work. A gradual ascension is best.

Dealing with Criticism

There will be negative nattering. Don't listen to it. Focus on the positive aspects of remote work instead. And keep in mind that there are already millions of people out there who live, thrive, and communicate in a fully digital world. Just ask anyone with a Facebook, Instagram, Twitter, or LinkedIn account.

And don't listen to leaders who say remote work will be bad

for business. The leaders at companies like Asana, DoorDash, Instacart, and Zoom (the list goes on and on) obviously didn't get that memo. Remote work will strengthen the national and global economic infrastructure in ways we never imagined. Embrace the positive. Kick the naysayers to the curb.

However, we must remember to be patient with employees as we navigate these still-turbulent waters of remote work and employees struggle to gain a solid foothold. *It will take time.* Until they are comfortable, employees will complain. Listen to their concerns and consider whether any improvements to the remote working system might be made.

It's taken generation after generation, lifetime after lifetime, to get to the point where we are today in our modern-day workforce. We have evolved in almost unimaginable ways since our parents, grandparents, and even great-grandparents made their contributions to the American workforce. Look at how much we have learned! And much of what have learned has been from the mistakes and missteps we and others before us have made, which is a positive thing, not a negative!

Imagine, two or three generations from today, where our workforce will be. Imagine the advancements we will have made. We stand at a precipice of change unlike any other we have encountered. As leaders, it is our duty, our responsibility, and it should be our *desire* to fly into the future fully armed with the tools and resources we need to keep our companies competitive, our employees fully engaged, our communities healthy and thriving, and the world itself moving in new directions.

Where we stand today is different than where we will stand tomorrow, and we must make the way for future leaders to step in and continue this momentum. We will not be leaders forever.

But at least for today, we are in a beautifully unique position to change the world.

Let's make sure we do it. And let's make sure we do it *right*.

8

The Virtuous Circle of Leadership

AS WE'VE JOURNEYED THROUGH THIS book together, you are now familiar with much of my personal and professional trajectory. You already know about my ascension into the digital world . . . and I use the word "ascension" deliberately because it feels like my transition from the traditional brick-and-mortar workplace to a fully digital space actually elevated my potential and placed me on a far more efficient "flight path."

I've shared with you that my move into the digital space grew, primarily, out of my own need to spend more time at home, taking care of myself, taking care of my family, and harnessing my energy as efficiently as possible so that I could face and fight my illness and restore myself to full health. What I didn't realize, when I got to GitLab, was that the experience working for such a cutting-edge company and stepping into the digital world would ignite within me a fire so intense that it continues to burn to this very moment. What I didn't realize was the extent to which the world of remote work would touch every aspect of my life and give me an extraordinary, reinvigorated sense of place and purpose. I *need* purpose in my life. We all do.

The small flame that burned within me all those years ago burns even brighter today. I hope to continue to spread its light wherever and however I can. Now that I have seen with my own eyes what remote work can do for people, for companies, for communities, and for the world itself, I *must* pay it forward. I *must* try to do everything within my power to make people aware of the limitless opportunities that exist in this world of remote work.

The fact that you are holding this book in your hands right now tells me that you have at least some interest in change, some desire to evolve into the kind of leader who can move in a new direction and guide people along a new path in order to change the world for the better. You're the kind of leader who is willing to change and adapt *even when it's uncomfortable*, because you know that it will be the change itself that will move us forward, together, to a more positive, more prosperous place where our lives and our work can become more impactful. This is the concept I want to pay forward. How could I not?

I've spent quite a bit of time bringing this principle to as many people as I possibly can, particularly those in the HR space, so that they, too, can pay it forward. That is what "paying it forward" is all about: generating positive momentum that transfers from one person, leader, or community to the next, in a way that brings about positive change for all of us. Isn't that the kind of leader you want to be?

I will admit that bringing the message of expanded opportunity by way of remote work has not been easy. I was singing this anthem *well* before the arrival of the global pandemic and, I'll be honest, the lyrics have not always fallen on receptive ears. New tunes are often difficult to hear. We tend to prefer the old stuff—the golden oldies.

Today, though, given the fact that *all* of us have used the technology available to switch to remote work (on some level anyway, just to survive), the song has become more palatable, the melody more familiar, the lyrics more easily remembered, which is definitely a good thing. But we've got a long way to go before we get to the place of full acceptance. I will continue singing this song. I will not stop. It is my Passion Song.

I remember speaking at my very last in-person conference, shortly before America started to shut down. I was speaking before a group of HR professionals. Of course, none of us could have predicted the intensity of the firestorm that was already raging towards us in the form of this highly transmissible disease that would wipe out so many lives. We didn't know that the world was about to change forever, which made my remarks that day even more fortuitous.

I wanted to make a point about the wonders and benefits of remote work. These were seasoned HR professionals, after all, who might be somewhat receptive to the message that they needed to start thinking about their workforces differently. I remember at one point while I was standing on the stage, I looked down at my watch and simply said, "Ninety-six." The audience was silent, confused by my numerical reference. I looked down my watch and said it again, to enhance the dramatic impact, "Ninety-six."

By this time, audience members were glancing around at each other inquisitively and looking at me expectantly as they tried to figure out where I was going with the repeated recitation of this single number. I brought it home for them, though. "It took me ninety-six minutes to get here to speak to you for a total of thirty minutes. Does that make logical sense?" I asked. "Is this the most efficient method of interacting and communicating? Is there another alternative? Let me answer that for you. Yes!"

I've had many moments like that on stage, trying to bring the message of remote work to those who are in a position to expand opportunity in the workplace, and I hope to have many more, because this is how I must pay it forward. This is how I must make a difference in the world.

How will *you* make a difference? How will you pay it forward, as a leader, in a way that helps your people grow, develop, and evolve into their very best selves? And how can you do this humbly and honorably, yet with strength, compassion, and unwavering dedication to not just your company but to the humans who comprise your company?

My passion, my *super* passion, happens to be remote work, but there are other passions I possess that I am committed to spreading and sharing, simply because I believe they make the world a better place. All of the leadership principles, traits, and characteristics that we've explored in this book, for instance. These are my passions: teaching people to lead with honor; teaching young leaders to never, ever give up, even when the road is rough and the chips are down; encouraging executives to embrace change and to lean into this fast-evolving world in a way that positions their companies to be stronger, better, more competitive; and spreading the good word about remote work and expanded opportunity simply because it touches *all* of us, at every level and in every capacity, in ways that we've explored in earlier chapters.

As we come to the finale of our literary journey, and as you begin to internalize and assimilate all of these leadership principles into your own daily lives, also begin to give some thought to how you, as a leader and a human, can pay your own passions forward.

> Have you been successful in your efforts thus far? What can you do to create a new momentum that allows you pay it forward with a greater sense of urgency, particularly given that the world is in such dire need of this positive momentum right now? How can you help your employees identify, explore, and then tap into their own passions, whatever they are, in a way that helps them feel seen? Heard? Valued? Respected? All of these are questions that I hope you will let rest in your heart … but don't let them rest too long. At some point, you must propel them into motion, because without motion, well, we are standing still.

There are so many ways you can make a positive difference in your company, in the lives of your employees, and in the communities you serve, but I have no doubt you've already made substantial positive difference in the world because you're a leader, and this is what leaders *do*.

The Marvel of Mentoring

Most, if not all, of us have benefited from having a mentor in our lives to guide, support, encourage, and even protect us when necessary. We wouldn't be where we are today without having had someone take us under their wing, steer us away from danger, and "show us how it's done." We stand on the shoulders of those who came before us; it is their path we trod, their wisdom we have reaped. How have *you* been guided and encouraged along the way? How have you reached back and expressed gratitude to those who once paved the way for you? Who protected and guided you? Are you content with how you are guiding, encouraging, and mentoring your work teams?

Even though we are poised to step into a bright new world, it is our mentors' lessons we will take with us. This is the value of creating support systems, of nurturing human connections based on trust, kindness, respect, honor, and dignity. There is so much value in mentorship.

Mentoring is also an ideal way to pay it forward. We must look at mentoring as a constant effort, rather than a one-time act. *Never let up*, no matter how far up you ascend. In fact, the further you ascend, the more time you should devote to helping others advance their own careers. It's a beautiful cycle; one helps another. We are each responsible for maintaining the cycle's momentum by mentoring.

Mentoring can unfold at every level of a person's career. We shouldn't make the assumption that mentoring is reserved for the younger employees. Although there is clear value in mentoring our youth, too often we forget the fact that even the mid-level manager could benefit from a steady, guiding hand and even the senior executive could use guidance, encouragement, and support. And the beauty of mentoring is that the relationship can grow over time. It doesn't have to be, and should not be, a one-off, flash-in-the-pan occurrence. It must endure.

What I share next is probably an extreme example of how a mentor-mentee relationship has been sustained, but I'll use it anyway because it also paints a rich portrait of how two employees, initially in the same company, formed a deep, trusting bond that still exists to this day.

Jessica worked for me for more than twenty years at different companies. She worked for me at Cisco, GitLab, and ClickUp. She started in an entry-level position and worked her way up, quickly and efficiently, because she happens to be extraordinarily bright and highly talented. I took Jessica under my wing because I saw things in her that shone like diamonds in the rough: commitment, strength, integrity, grit, tenacity, brilliance. In fact, every single trait and characteristic that we have explored in this book I saw, with my own eyes, in Jessica.

Over so many years, as I mentioned, we have developed a relationship of incredible trust and respect. I was always glad to see her ascend, and help her ascend, to higher positions because she deserved it, and because it brought great value to the companies we worked for. A win-win. As she advanced, never once did I feel protective of my position. Never once did I feel intimated or threatened by seeing her star rise as beautifully and as steadily as it did. In fact, I once pointed out to her that she kept following me from job to job, when she could conceivably and fairly easily *replace* me! The truth of the matter is that we must help each other grow and make sure we do all we can to see each other's stars rise—even if that star ultimately rises higher than ours.

This is what great leaders *do*! They surround themselves with people who are just as smart (or smarter) than they are, and they do everything in their power to help those people become the very best version of themselves they can possibly be. *That* is paying it forward. I strongly believe that Jessica will do the same for other employees as she continues to ascend. In fact, I know she already has because I've seen her in action. Positive momentum creates positive momentum. The cycle perpetuates. We must do everything in our power to ensure that the momentum remains strong and sure and constant.

In the mentoring arena, I also make it a point of speaking to students at Santa Clara University (my alma mater) on a fairly regular basis, usually the MBA and undergrad students. I do it because I want to invest in them, show them that there are people and professionals out there who believe in them and who believe in the good that they will one day bring into the world. And I will be honest: from a recruiting perspective, it's also helpful to me to be able to see the talent that's about to enter the job market. And the fact that some of these students have chosen to go into the field of human resources makes me particularly proud.

My hope is that, one day, they too will pay it forward by returning to their alma mater to keep the positive momentum going. I did it. Those before me did it. I have total faith in the generation about to be unleashed onto the world, that they will continue the cycle at Santa Clara. What would happen if they *didn't* is not a rosy picture at all. With dedication, constant effort, and purposeful intention, the cycle will remain unbroken.

Message for the Young:
This Stuff Isn't Easy

Whenever I speak to young people, which is fairly often—whether it's at my kids' school's Career Development Day or to new hires or to young entrepreneurs—I am always honest and straightforward with this message: success takes hard work. Period. If you don't put in the time, you won't reap the rewards of success. It isn't easy, by any means, but putting in the hard work is *necessary* if you want to win the race.

There is another part to this message that I am also careful to include. I tell them that it's not just putting in the effort that will bring success. Heck, lots of people put in a gargantuan effort and never see success. Ultimately, it's also about being able *to achieve the desired results.* Hard work combined with achieving the desired outcome, whether that outcome is scoring the winning touchdown, turning in the strongest profit-earnings statement, or sealing that deal with a big new client. Hard work + desired result = victory. That is the winning combination. No two ways about it.

What is also important for young people to remember is that their success is not and should not be tied to external circumstances, such as who you know or what you look like or how you happen to identify. Your success depends on the work you put in and the results you achieve: nothing more, nothing less. And even then, even when they do get this combination right, the dream of "having it all" is simply not realistic. I never try to dash their dreams, of course, but I am always truthful. My message is this: *you cannot have it all, but you can have what you want the most.*

If everyone were to pay it forward *all the time*, if we all—you, me, your colleague in accounting, the upper-middle manager who was just promoted to the C-suite—took it upon ourselves to constantly perpetuate this cyclical momentum without letting up, we wouldn't even *need* mentoring programs! If each of us held ourselves personally and professionally accountable for paying it forward and everyone took ownership of both this principle and this practice, we could remove the word "mentor" from our vocabulary. There would be no need to create groups, platforms, and organizations that are dedicated to helping others, simply because it would already be woven into the fabric of our leadership lives. It would already be a principle that we lived by each and every day, as a reflex rather than a sense of obligation. If this were the case, mentoring would not need to be mandated.

Isn't this what we want to aspire to? A world where mentoring, paying it forward, and creating positive momentum is a normal part of our daily lives? A constant part of our human experience? A consistent characteristic in our lives as leaders?

If our goal is to expand opportunity (and expanding opportunity is the most effective and efficient way to "pay it forward" for all people), then why aren't we moving with a stronger sense of urgency?

9

The Future Is Now!

WHEN LEADERS TALK ABOUT THE future, when we plan for how our companies will evolve and how we will lead them into these next stages of being, there's something we should remember: the future is not decades down the road or light years away. It is not waiting to be decrypted, decoded, or dissected in Silicon Valley, Los Alamos, or Bell Labs. It is not nestled between the pages of some new and unfathomable science fiction novel. It's not waiting for us patiently in a petri dish in an upstairs lab at Harvard Medical School or in a basement bunker at MIT. That's not where the future is. The future is right here. *It is now.*

The future lies in your hands—in *our* hands—and it is up to us to shepherd our employees and our companies straight into it with courage, with grace, with determination, and with no hesitation.

The future (something we thought was far off), as we have already explored in earlier chapters, reached right out slapped us square in our faces during the pandemic, then it dragged us kicking and screaming into the world of remote work. So, in a very real way, we have already seen the face of the future … and the future is now. This digital work world is the face of the future. This is the world we live in, and the world we live in is only moving forward. Life is incapable of moving backward—only humans can move in reverse, time cannot.

Younger generations have now become accustomed to working remotely. They appreciate, value, and perhaps even cherish this newfound freedom and this sudden, almost infinite expansion of opportunity. They have already tasted the sweet nectar of the future, i.e., working in a fully digital environment and being able to work where they *live*, and they have already begun to reap the social, financial, and emotional rewards that come from living in this New World. They will not be going back to the old model. And if you want to remain competitive, neither should you. Resist the urge to go back to the old ways of leading and living. Don't return to the "what was" just because the pandemic robbed us of the ability to fully enjoy the benefits of remote work. The only option is to bravely face "what will one day be." You get to choose.

The past has already been lived. There is nothing there for you, nothing there for your employees, nothing there for the future of the company that you lead. There are other options; you have *seen* these options, so you know they work. Indeed, the pandemic propelled us forward. At what other time in our history have we been catapulted into another way of living and working with such catastrophic force and fury? Yes, the force itself was catastrophic, but what we *do* with that force and how we *build* on this momentum, now that we have it, does not have to be catastrophic at all. What we do now, where we go from here, can be as radical and as revelatory as we *choose* it to be. That's the thing: the choice is not just within our reach. *It is in our hands.*

Also understand this. Our next steps will define, or at least usher in, an entire era of new, young leaders. Don't we want to usher them in responsibly? As the senior managers and seasoned executives that we are, don't we want to exit stage left when it's our time in a way that invites new leaders to take our place and become the best new leaders they can possibly be? Don't we want to teach them how to eventually create their own leadership legacies so that they, too, when the time comes, can usher in those even younger leaders who are already gathering in the wings?

Remember that this is cyclical momentum we are creating here; the same concept we talked about in the previous chapter. This is not just about remote work. Remote work is a vital part of this cycle, obviously, and this concept of expanded opportunity is what lies at the center of this cycle, but the cycle itself is far larger than that. It's about much, much more. This is about creating a world that is vastly, boldly, audaciously different from the world we know today. But changes of his magnitude, on this vast a scale, will take time. This stuff is multi-generational. We cannot even fathom what changes will occur in the workplace and the world in the years, decades, and generations to come, but what we *do* know, with clarity and conviction, is this: right here and right now is when we step into the future. We must usher it in. We must set the stage. It is our obligation, our responsibility.

As we evaluate what comes next, we must evaluate the state of things and the state of things to come with a clear-eyed sensibility, one that is rooted in reality rather than in the gauzy, amorphous dreams of yesterday. Rather, we must operate from a place of authentic truth. We must hold ourselves and each other accountable—this is what will ensure that we continue to lead our employees with the traits and characteristics we have explored throughout this book: integrity, character, courage to change, and the constant desire to tell the truth, even if that truth is painful and uncomfortable.

One truth that is absolute and unyielding, particularly as it concerns the principle and practice of expanded opportunity in the world and the workplace, is this: Not every company will exercise the option to step into a completely virtual workplace, but you can bet your bottom dollar that every individual given the option of working remotely will certainly exercise that option! Why? Because they know, now, that have the option to *choose*. In almost the twinkling of an eye, that choice has been presented to them. They have tasted the nectar. They will not be turning back.

Of course, there are some professionals whose financial wherewithal depends on human contact, such as those in the service and hospitality industry (hair stylists, restaurant workers, etc.), those in public safety roles (police officers, firefighters, etc.), and those in the medical field (doctors, nurses, etc.). But even for those professionals who depend upon human contact and direct interaction, though, the news is good. The news is *great*, actually. Because more people will be working where they live, they will be funneling their income back into their local communities. This means the corner café in your neighborhood will have more patrons. It means the local doctor just around the block will have more patients. It means the employees at the front desk of your local community center will be there every morning to unlock the doors and open the center to those who are waiting to step inside to gather, swim, read, exercise, whatever they choose to do in their community center! It means the hair stylist, who recently set up shop in the new neighborhood strip mall and the bookstore owner just around the corner will now have a steady stream of regular clients in need of their services. *It means that communities can come alive again.*

As we explored in the last two chapters, communities will be revived, reinvigorated, and renewed, not from gentrification, which occurs when you have outside people coming in and displacing the old, but from *revitalization*, which occurs when the people who were originally born and raised in these communities can now take advantage of the opportunity to stay where they are, to work where they are, to live and raise families and play in the same parks they played in when they were children. Why? Because they no longer have to spend an hour or two commuting from home to office, office to home, which means they will have more time for living, for loving, for dining out, for staying in, for spending time with family and friends, for simply *being*. People will no longer be required to leave their communities because their jobs demand it. Coast-to-coast relocations and mandatory transfers will no longer be a part of the paradigm; people can work where they live.

Where do I see us going in the future? Towards communities that are closer and more cohesive. Towards neighborhoods, enclaves, and cul-de-sacs that still have the comfortable, collective pulse and heartbeat of the families that have been living there for generations. I see the fabric of communities being sewn back together after having been fragmented for so long.

With expanded opportunity for more people—with the technology and software companies driving this change, primarily—I see less "zip code disparity." No longer will those who live in affluent communities be the only ones who have access to continued growth and enrichment. Opportunity will now be able to find you wherever you live; it will come to you. You will not have to get to it (providing you have the skills, the talent, the drive, and the desire to work hard and produce good, solid results in your remote workspace).

I see a world where it is not *wealth* we are trying to spread, but opportunity itself. Opportunity and education are the great equalizers.

Remote Work = Growth

You've no doubt seen this workforce trend already unfolding. Perhaps it's happening in your state right now. State and local governments are bending over backward to try to attract new workers. Pulling out all the stops.

Whether they're launching ambitious new advertising campaigns that depict their state as the best state in the nation to live and work, or whether they're offering financial incentives to attract new workers ("We'll offer you a $10,000 tax incentive to move to our state!"), this much is clear: state and local governments want a piece of this highly lucrative "remote work" pie.

They *see* how this increased flexibility, freedom, and unlimited mobility is giving wage-earners more choice (particularly the younger wage-earners), and states are eager to capitalize on these expanded choices. What this tells us is that remote work is creating tremendous economic growth in a way that has never been seen before.

Again, everyone wins. The only ones who *don't* win are those companies and those leaders who are too frightened, or too hesitant, or too skeptical, or too stuck in their own ways to step with the rest of the world into this exciting new future.

How will we step together, as humans who coexist on this singular planet, into this evolving new world? How will we lead in a way that promotes positive change, not just in the workplace but in the world? What was once thrust upon us against our will by a deadly virus is now the best option for growth (or the potential for growth) and advancement.

As we stand at this precipice, the decisions we make and the actions we take are completely within our control. This part bears repeating: this time around, we have control; this time around, we have a *choice*. We must move forward.

The rest of the world will move forward. Staying stuck in the past is foolish. Refusing to change because change is uncomfortable is audaciously irresponsible.

> Remember that the less we change, the less we are capable of change.

We are leaders, so the desire and the capacity to change must live within us, as well as our desire and capacity to *choose*.

What kinds of choices will you be brave enough, bold enough, and audacious enough to make moving forward? In which direction will you move? When it boils down to it, you have three choices.

The first choice is to move forward.

The second choice is to move backward.

The third choice is to stand still.

If you want to survive, if you want your employees, your company, your organizational culture, your communities, and the world around you to thrive, the last two options are not really options at all. Only one wise choice remains:

Move forward with the rest of us.

Now.

10

Push Past Boundaries

ALTHOUGH WE HAVE ARRIVED SO quickly, it seems, at the end of our journey together here, our leadership journey is only just beginning. I do hope you can feel the connection we've made as we have explored these leadership principles and concepts together. *I* feel the connection. For me, anyway, the connection is powerful. Palpable. It has a pulse. It is real.

What this tells me, and what I hope it tells you, is that our capacity to connect to each other as human beings is virtually limitless. We do not have to be in the same room, or even on the same continent, to share ideas and exchange information in a meaningful and enduring way. No matter where we are in the world, we are bound together by our shared humanity and a strong sense of collective purpose.

Before this book was brought into existence, there was no

pre-existing relationship between us, but now that this door of communication has been opened. Now that we have traveled together on this leadership journey, we have placed ourselves on a common leadership path. We've explored many different leadership principles and practices, evaluating and reflecting upon them in a way that will hopefully allow you to incorporate them into your own life. Which direction you choose to go from here is up to you; which of these leadership principles you decide to honor, practice, and propel forward into your corporate culture and your collective communities is your choice. Whichever direction you take, though, remember that you will not be taking it alone.

We are a community of leaders. A country of leaders. A wide and wonderful *world* of leaders, now bound together by technology so advanced that we can leapfrog over continents, share our talent and resources in ways that we've never shared before, and purposefully contribute to the process of making the world a better, kinder, more efficient, happier, and more human-centered place. As we step into this exciting, scary, intimidating, wildly amazing new future before us, we will step together. And as we do, the world will change.

Leaders push past boundaries. We create new conduits and connections. We guide our teams and grow our people in a way that brings benefit to them, to our companies, and to the wider world around us. That's pretty heady stuff, when you think about it, and a *very* tall order, but we are up to the task. *You* are up the task. You wouldn't be where you are today, having enjoyed the success and upward mobility you have already enjoyed (and no doubt richly deserve), were you not up to the task.

Whether you're a new businessowner, a seasoned executive, a recent college grad, or simply a human being out here in the world trying your best to make a positive impact in your community, the most important thing to remember is that the task and the responsibility of creating expanded opportunity belongs to all of us.

We must hold each other accountable, turn to each other for support, rely upon each other for guidance and encouragement, and constantly develop new ways to help our people grow. Much of their growth will come from being allowed to live and work within their own communities (whenever possible and feasible). And understand this: Forcing them to make a choice between one or the other, between living in one place and working in another, is no longer responsible; not when there *can* be a choice.

Pebbles in the Pond

This brings us gracefully back to the pebble-in-the-pond concept that has featured consistently throughout this book. When we empower our employees and teams by *purposefully expanding their opportunity*, i.e., affording them the opportunity to work where they live, we are helping to enrich every single aspect of their lives. We are allowing them to deepen their human connections. We are redefining our corporate culture in a way that invites and facilitates greater diversity, inclusion, and a collective sense of belonging. We are dropping that all-important pebble in the pond, creating all *kinds* of waves that will spread outward and wash over countless communities, countless cultures, and countless human lives. We hold that precious pebble in our hands; let's drop it responsibly.

As we arrive at the closing chapter of this book, I also want to reflect, again, on the trajectory of the book itself. I'd like to close where we opened; to finish at the point where we started.

At the beginning of the book, you'll remember that I reflected on how the idea of this book began as a love letter I wrote long ago to my children. Not just a love letter, though; I was also writing a *goodbye* letter. As I wrote to my two children, I knew that there was a high probability that I would not live to see them grow into adults. I would not be around to walk them to school or see them graduate from college or watch them get married and have children. I would not have the opportunity to be a mother to them, much less a grandmother to my yet unborn grandchildren. When I wrote those letters to my children, I wanted to leave them with lessons and with my enduring-but-humble wisdom about how to live life meaningfully, how to be kind to others, how to connect with the world around them, how to be happy, and how to create happiness for the humans surrounding them.

It was upon those same principles that this very book is based— proof positive that life and leadership really are one and the same thing. When within our organizations we practice kindness, help others grow, refuse to fear change or give up, and pay it forward, remember that these are also all things we should be doing in our lives and our communities. No matter where we are or what we're doing or who we're leading (and we're always leading, supporting, or impacting *someone* in some capacity, whether we know it or not), these are the principles we must fight for and uphold.

Looking back on it now, I realize that I wasn't just writing those goodbye letters to my children for my children: I was writing them for myself, too. The exercise of writing the letters helped me understand, appreciate, and embrace the fact that we all have wisdom to share.

> We all have lessons to leave and *wisdom that deserves to endure.*

And if we don't capture this wisdom in some way, if we don't record it or write it down or preserve it in some manner, we simply will not be able to pass it along. Whatever is worth being passed along must first be *preserved.* The act of preservation is a step we often miss.

The same principle holds true in leadership, too. If we do not act with purpose to preserve and pass along the experiential wisdom that we know is worthy of being shared, the wisdom will eventually lose its momentum. It will fizzle out. It will wither away and die. We must create forums that allow us to communicate with each other clearly and consistently. We must make mechanisms that allow the best of who we are to endure, long after we ourselves have taken our leave.

And we must also embrace the fact that we lead *multitudes.* Wherever we go, we are leaders. Our role as leader does not disappear or dissipate. *It moves where we move.* When we move about in our community, we are influencing others in some way. At the grocery store, the gas station, even in the neighborhood coffee shop, the principles that we practice (kindness, respect, dignity, honor)—qualities that make us the best versions of ourselves we can possibly be—are what help make this world a better place.

I want to repeat this again: the leadership qualities and characteristics we possess belong to us all the time. They move where we move in a way that almost mirrors of the concept of remote work itself, which moves where we move. This is both a comforting and an awe-inspiring realization. It is simultaneously joyous and sobering, because it reminds us that we must be responsible stewards moving forward.

As we live and work in the world, we never fully realize how much of an influence we truly have on others. Whether the influence we wield is positive or negative is totally up to us; it is bound and defined by our behavior. The very fact that we do not fully realize the scope of our influence on others is itself a reminder that we must *always* be kind, *always* be honorable, *always* move forward with courage and confidence. We never know who might be looking. We never know who might be in need of our inspiration and guidance. We never know who might need a random act of kindness, given freely, from you or from me.

I think about the young lady who reached out to me on Facebook some years ago, not too long after Facebook took the world by storm. It was a time when everybody was searching for (and finding) old friends, connecting and re-connecting with each other, utilizing the social media platform in a way that would eventually change the world as we know it. As it turned out, this young lady had gone to high school with me. She used the technology at her disposal to find me and communicate with me after all those years. She wrote me a long message about how difficult high school had been for her and how hard it had been to adjust, fit in, and survive. It felt isolating for her to always have stood on the fringes of all the social circles, never invited to sit with the anyone in the cafeteria. She went on to say that she was writing to me, after all these years, to thank me for being so kind to her during that difficult time. She thanked me for always recognizing her. For always seeing her. For always treating her with dignity, respect, and warmth. She told me what a difference it made to her then, and what a difference the memory makes to her now.

Did I realize, back then, that my kindness would have such a positive and lasting impact on her? Of course I didn't! I confess that I never made the concerted effort to *be* kind; I was just a typical, head-in-the-sky high school kid, after all. I'm also a little ashamed to admit that I don't remember the young lady who reached out to me on Facebook; nevertheless, this is proof positive that the kindness and decency we carry within us can, and does, endure. It goes where we go. It doesn't dissipate or disappear. It washes over other people in ways we can never fully anticipate. Her reaching out, in fact, has impacted the leader I am today. It made me question my actions of the past, and it steered me towards committing to do better in the future. Experiences like these can (and should) impact not just our lives as leaders but also our overall understanding of how we must treat each other at all times, in all circles, across every space and spectrum of life. Life is leadership. Leadership is life.

Now that we have established a bond of sorts within the pages of this book, let's make sure that we push these written words out into the world in a way that creates maximum impact. Drop the pebble, so to speak.

To do this, join me at barbiejane.com, as we establish a forum that allows us to stay connected to each other. To communicate, to commiserate (occasionally), to call on each other when we need to, and to celebrate each other's advancement and growth as we continue to build our leadership muscles.

I would love to hear how you have been able to weave the principles we've explored in this book into the fabric of your life as a leader and a human. How have you used these tools and techniques to strengthen the human connections in your community and within your organization? How will you communicate these concepts to your team in a way that is most meaningful and impactful? What resources will you rely upon—internal and external resources alike—to help advance this new leadership journey?

*

Now that we have been given the tools, now that we have explored the options, now that we have established a leadership bond that helps strengthen and define our sense of collective purpose moving forward, we must remember that the changes we are about to make are not only within our reach . . . they are already *in our hands.*

The choice is ours.
The world is waiting.
Change it we must.

www.barbiejane.com/LeadandLetLive

ACKNOWLEDGMENTS

IN WRITING THIS BOOK, I recognized that I have been influenced by many of the people in my life. I will never be able to do justice to those who have positively impacted my life. If you don't see your name here, you would see it in my heart.

I cannot help but start with my children, Kyle and Madeleine. They taught me to be a better leader. They taught me patience, elation, strength, resilience, and grit. They remind me that we all had to learn to walk before we could run, and to be unafraid to get back up and try again. Every day I see them learning something new, trying out for the team, being tested . . . I wish that as adults, we had the same eagerness and willingness to be bad at something, knowing we can learn and grow to be better. I love you kids and apologize for embarrassing you!

As you will have read in my book, my mom, Jeanne Bailey, has always been my rock, my lifelong supporter, and—along with my sister, Kathie Knudsen—my shoulder to lean on. Both have also always been willing to call me on my BS, which I definitely need more than I'm proud to admit. Needless to say, I wouldn't be here if it wasn't for my mom. But more than that, I am not sure what a crazy, risk-tasking, overactive, and strong-willed kid like me would have become without a mom who found the perfect balance in guiding, without restricting, my energy.

My husband, Greg Brewer, is the person who encouraged me most to write this book. He came into my life at a difficult time. I was a single mom battling, at first, an unknown illness and, soon after, a very rare tumor. He welcomed my kids and me into his life without hesitation and has stood by us through everything. I love and appreciate his support of me and willingness to love me when I'm not feeling lovable.

My friends have been a constant in my life, even at the times I can be quite absent. I will not begin to name each of you, but I hope you know who are. My friends from grade school: we may go years without seeing each other, but when we talk, it's like a single day hasn't passed. My friends from college, who saw me during my wild days and don't hold it against me: I love our annual holiday dinner and impromptu gatherings in between. My "mom friends": We may have met through our children, but our friendships have grown beyond sports games and mom's groups. I love that, as women, we support and accept each other: the good, the bad, and the ugly.

My work teammates, past and present: I have learned so much from each of you. Kate DeCamp, thank you for taking a chance on me. Patty McCord and Tawni Cranz, thank you for continuing my learning and opportunity. I have also been blessed to work with some of the best CEOs and leaders in their industries and have been inspired by them. I have been able to take those learnings to help the next generation of leaders. Unsurprisingly, I have learned just as much from those who have worked for me as those I have worked for. Each person I hire is better than me at what they do. Thank you for being a part of my teams, some of you at multiple companies! One day, I may be lucky enough to work for you.

Lastly, I want to thank my dogs. You relax me, are always happy to see me, and show true, unconditional love. I may be a crazy dog lady, but I'm glad I am!

ABOUT THE AUTHOR

BARBIE BREWER began her career in Silicon Valley during the dot.com boom of the '90s and is now an industry-leading expert in developing critical areas of modern business performance and culture, including remote and hybrid workforces.

As Chief Culture Officer at GitLab Inc., Brewer has contributed to the all-remote SAS company's growth from 150 employees to over 1,000 in more than 60 countries. She was Vice President of Talent for Netflix when the streaming service expanded from 20 million subscribers to over 150 million. As an advisory/interim HR leader, Brewer has worked with hypergrowth companies in Silicon Valley and New York to build out and coach the C-Suite. While at Cisco, she lived and worked in Europe for three years.

Brewer holds a Master's in Human Resource Management and a Bachelor's in Communication and Business from Santa Clara University.

While Brewer is passionate about her career and the future of work, she is most devoted to her two teenagers, a supportive husband, and four dogs. Love of family and recognition of the need for impactful leadership inspired her to write this book.